THE ROAD FROM WIGAN PIER

THE ROAD FROM WIGAN PIER

WIGAN ATHLETIC'S INCREDIBLE RISE FROM NON-LEAGUE TO THE PREMIERSHIP

dewi lewis media

For Christine, Tommy, Iain and Stuart

THE ROAD FROM WIGAN PIER
by Andrew Ross

This edition first published in the UK in 2007 by
Dewi Lewis Media Ltd
8, Broomfield Road
Heaton Moor
Stockport SK4 4ND
www.dewilewismedia.com

> Design and Artwork Production
Dewi Lewis Media Ltd, based on an original design concept
by Arco da Velha – Design e Ilustração, Lda, Portugal
Cover design from pictures of Wigan Atheletic Kits by
Bernard Ramsdale, Andy Werrill, Graham Millington &
www.yeoldetreeandcrown.34sp.com

> Print and binding
Biddles Ltd, Kings Lynn

ISBN: 978-1-905928-01-9

10   9   8   7   6   5   4   3   2   1

CONTENTS

FOREWORD   DAVE WHELAN

As a Wigan man and a football man it has been a dream come true for me to become involved with Wigan Athletic and see the club enjoy such success. I'm not sure that anyone else really believed when I took over the club that we could achieve what we have, but I never doubted it for a second. I never doubted it because when Wigan Athletic dominated non-League football in the 1950s, 60s and 70s at Springfield Park it was a great club. When it was languishing at the foot of the Football League on the verge of bankruptcy it was a great club. And when it scaled the League to reach the heady heights of the top three in the best league in the world it was an especially great club.

What makes Wigan Athletic the club it is are the people involved with it. Even in the club's darkest days just before I got involved the fans kept coming to matches, kept putting money in the dreaded collection buckets with as much enthusiasm as the people (like current chief executive Brenda Spencer) who did the collections week in week out just to make sure the club saw another day. At some stages it looked like it wouldn't. Thankfully it did and today Brenda is able to write £5m cheques for international players without hesitation. It's a sign of how far we've all come.

They say that the best thing about travelling is not the arriving but the journey itself. Some of our younger fans who've only known this as a top flight club may beg to differ but there are many fans on the terraces who value our current success precisely because they know how far we have come. And that journey is not over.

In our first season in the Premiership the club excelled. A top ten finish and a cup final appearance was an incredible return for a club that was tipped to go straight back down. It confirmed what I believed all along – that we've always been a Premiership club in waiting. There's never been a prouder moment in my life as when the team walked out at the Millennium Stadium for the Carling Cup final. We're all aware that that day could have ended better but – like this club always does – we'll learn from it, bounce back and do better next time.

And so to the present. As I write this we've just ended our difficult second season in the top flight. Survival was imperative but in the future we'll be striving to match our achievements of our debut season in the top flight.

Who's to say we can't do it? Not me. It was my dream to see the Latics in the Premiership, to see the likes of Arsenal, Chelsea, Liverpool and Manchester United come to the JJB Stadium. Now the club has got a taste for the big time I don't think any fan would like to see us go back to where we came from. As a fan I share those feelings.

Many of you will have your own memories of past Wigan sides, of past successes and failures but never before have all the highs and lows been collected in one book. Andrew Ross's fascinating telling of the history of the club in these pages should make Latics fans proud. I hope too that its fantastic journey from non-league to the Premiership will appeal to all football fans, not just those in Wigan. Indeed it should serve as a reminder to all football fans that the game is not just about big business. It is about people and about dreams. It should serve as inspiration for those involved with lower league clubs because in this brilliant game that is so often the subject of criticism anything is possible.

That is why this club and its fans should take enormous credit from where it is. Wigan Athletic is a decent, honest football club that even when it faced extinction dared to dream of a better day and has worked its socks off both on and off the field to realise that dream. It has been an honour to have been able to play my part and I envisage a long association between the Whelan family and the club.

Dave Whelan

FOREWORD   PAUL JEWELL

Wigan Athletic is a club that has been through the best of times and worst of times. I feel privileged that I have been able to contribute to the Latics's success over the years as both a player and as a manager as the club held its own in one of the best leagues in the world. Now they're in the top flight the hard work has only just begun. To stay up and become established as a force in the Premiership would be an incredible achievement but it is this challenge that drives the club forward.

Once people said that Wigan Athletic was not a Premiership club. If, in a couple of years, people start to think that they cannot imagine the club being anywhere else but the Premiership, challenging for honours, then and only then will the club have truly arrived.

At some points in my time there as manager it looked like we'd never make it that far. When I joined the club the potential there was evident. I couldn't believe how much it had changed from when I was a player. There was a new stadium, even a training ground – something we'd certainly never had in the 1980s when we had to fight over training kit – all paid for by a new chairman who was willing to invest in the club. Yet after a succession of managers in the previous seasons the club was in disarray.

As you read on you'll find that it didn't go well from the start but my assistant, and eventual successor, Chris Hutchings and I stuck to our task. We moved some players on who we thought didn't deserve to pull on the Wigan Athletic shirt. We brought in players who were willing to work hard, who wanted to do well for the club, for themselves and for each other. We wanted our players to embody the motto of this club: *Progress with Unity*. Slowly our fortunes improved. There was no quick fix, however, it was down to hard graft.

Looking back on my time at the club there are so many highpoints: winning the Nationwide Division Two with 100 points, beating Reading to win promotion to the top flight for the first time in the club's history, and conquering an Arsenal side that went all the way to the Champions League final, and so reach an historic Carling Cup final. Reading Andrew Ross's honest and compelling account of those times brings back some happy memories.

This book is not just about the good times, however. The club has had to fight tooth and nail to protect its League status at times and Ross has spoken to figures past and present – including players, managers, chairmen and fans – who played their part along the way. What emerges is a portrait of a club that worked hard, never gave up hope, and deserves its place amongst football's elite. Ross's book does justice to the tremendous history of this club and its journey from non-league to the Premiership. It is a must-read for any football fan.

Paul Jewell

PROLOGUE

It's November 19, 2005. The time, 12.45pm. The location, somewhere in the North West of England. The setting, a stunning 25,000 seater state-of-the-art stadium. The ground is full to the brim, the official attendance that day is 25,004. For this is a must-see showdown between two of the Barclays Premiership's high flyers. Two of the top teams in the best league in the world are set to do battle.

The home team are defending a nine match unbeaten run which in recent weeks has seen them claim the scalps of Everton, Bolton, Newcastle, Aston Villa and Fulham, conceding a solitary goal in the process. The run has seen them climb to second in the table, just behind champions Chelsea. By the end of the day Manchester United will have climbed up to third, just ahead of today's visitors, Arsenal, in fourth.

It's a frantic first half and after 21 minutes the London side are already two nil up courtesy of goals from Dutch international Robin Van Persie and French World Cup winner Thierry Henry. It's heady stuff and the home team look dead and buried. But then the fight back begins. First the home side's record £3.1m signing, one of a new breed of international stars at the club, pulls one back. It's game on until Henry pops up on 41 minutes to put the visitors 3-1 up with a stunning free kick. But the home team refuse to lie down. With the half time whistle about to sound, the midfielder, who joined the club for £275,000 when it was in Nationwide League Division Two just three years before, skips past England defender Sol Campbell as if he's not there and curls a left foot shot past the stranded German national keeper, Jens Lehmann.

At half time the crowd can barely wait for the goal fest to restart. Some fans wander off to buy a coffee and one of the pies the town is famous for. Some jump up and down to get some feeling back in their frozen limbs while others sit motionless, scanning the match day programme. The *Once Upon A Time* section in the programme would certainly have made interesting reading, recalling a match from 1994, eleven years ago to the very day. The league: Endsleigh League Division Three, the lowest of the four in the Football League, the home side having just been relegated there the season before.

But with a new manager the 1994 team was resurgent. Having just weeks earlier been rock bottom of the 92 teams in the Football League and on the brink of financial ruin, they were fighting back, calling on all the inner strength that they had – on every single player, every staff member, and every single one of the 1,500 fans who turned out to watch them in the decrepit, empty stadium. It was a time to live up to the club motto, *Progress with Unity*, and drag the club back from the abyss.

Halftime that day in 1994 during the match with Darlington couldn't have been nearly as much fun for the fans as it was in 2005. Now, fans could watch the halftime entertainment, the club's lottery draw, the cheerleaders, even an opera singer, exchange light hearted banter with the genteel away support, and look forward to seeing their team recommence battle with an Arsenal side that would come within a whisker of winning the Champions League later that season.

In 1994 as the meagre crowd headed to buy their halftime refreshments after watching a scrappy first half in an empty stadium they would have been accosted by the club's chief executive shaking a collection bucket. And this was no raffle or charity collection. It was for the players' wages. Things were grave and every fan dug deep into their pockets, some forgoing their halftime pint so they could pop a couple more pounds into the buckets that had rattled around the stadium at every home match in recent memory. One day the buckets would be banished from the terraces for good leaving an eerie, unnatural silence in the dilapidated ground. Sometime later the silence would be replaced by applause and singing as fans returned to the terraces in their droves. But for the time-being Wigan Athletic were on the brink.

A 4-1 victory that day lifted the club out of the bottom three at the wrong end of the Football League on goal difference only. It was bleak. Bleak too was having had seven managers in the previous ten years. Bleak was seeing the best team the club had ever had being sold off one by one to keep the bailiffs from the door. Bleak was having to ask the 1,500 loyal fans who came to your every match to put their hand in their pockets each and every time so the club could put out a team the following Saturday.

Being 3-2 down at halftime in a top of the table Premiership clash against one of the best teams on the planet, a team they'd conquer just two months later to clinch an historic place in the final of the Carling Cup, wasn't bleak. It was like a birthday present compared to where the club had come from.

1 EARLY BEGINNINGS

That Wigan Athletic's promotion to the Premiership for the 2005/06 season and the club's tremendous effort to maintain their Premiership status since is a lofty achievement is in no doubt. In ten short years the club has gone from skid row, propping up the bottom of the Football League and on the verge of bankruptcy, to millionaires' row, proudly sitting (in the 2005/06 season at least) alongside the Chelseas and Manchester Uniteds of this world, competing for silverware and European places.

More of that later, much more. What is less well known is that but for the sheer grit and determination of a handful of people from Wigan in the latter parts of the 19th Century and early 20th Century it is probable that no football whatsoever would be played in the town today. Wigan Athletic's story is not just about a small town football club which struggled for years in the lower reaches of the League before being rescued by a local multimillionaire. Wigan's story is considerably more complex than that. And though 'Latics' fans everywhere owe a massive debt of gratitude to the club's founding fathers for their persistence, the after effects of these footballing pioneers' early, faltering attempts to establish a foothold for the game in the town were to ring out for years to come with devastating effect.

Just to set the record straight: Wigan Athletic FC can trace its roots back at least as far as the famous rugby league club with which it today shares an uneasy truce and a stadium – a little known fact in what is seen, much to the annoyance of Latics fans everywhere, as a 'rugby town'. But it is a fact that should be etched into the psyche of each and every one of the 4,000 young Latics season ticket holders today. Then, and only then, can the misconception that rugby rules the small Lancashire town be laid to rest.

The first traceable rudimentary 'dribbling football' played in the town was by members of a club known simply as 'Wigan'. It is thought the first organised game took place sometime in early 1873 but this was still a full ten years before the Football Association (FA) published its first rule book. By then, with Wigan long since disbanded, Wigan AFC, the first real identifiable club in the Wigan Athletic family tree, had been formed.

Accounts from the time highlighted how Wigan AFC's popularity grew so quickly that local rugby clubs had to offer free tickets to win fans back from the fast growing, exciting Association Football. Despite the growing enthusiasm for the game, come the 1888/89 season the club had hit the skids. Lessons were learnt from the club's failure, not least that a permanent home for the club was a prerequisite for stability and success.

It was not until the FA updated its Association rules in December 1896 that football was truly to take a hold on the town. Wigan County FC, formed soon after, was to be the first football team in the town to play at Springfield Park and thus the club most fans recognise as Wigan Athletic's truest ancestor.

County meant business from the outset. The club's ambition was to one day gain access to the Football League, a target that was seen as almost as unattainable as Dave Whelan's claim that he'd take Wigan Athletic to the Premiership from the foot of the Football League within ten years of taking over. It seems that Wigan teams always thought big.

The 1898/99 season saw County become the first senior Wigan football team to bring home any silverware – the Rawcliffe Charity Cup – and, buoyed by the success, they made an audacious application to join the Football League for the first time. Despite receiving votes from seven clubs in the ballot, it wasn't to be.

Wigan's failure to gain access to the League did not come as a surprise. If there was one thing the gentlemen that comprised the League committee didn't like it was teams with chequered pasts. For Wigan to improve its chances of accession to the League it would have to prove that football had gained a firm and lasting place in the hearts and minds of the local populace.

The club's ambition was to one day gain access to the Football League

County enjoyed two good years at Springfield Park regularly playing in front of crowds of up to 4,000. But all was not as it seemed. After struggling to honour their league commitments as the 1899/1900 season progressed, the second-from-bottom club went under. Though County were the latest in a succession of failed senior football teams in the town, the sport had put down some solid foundations. However, with rugby vying for the hard-earned cash of Wiganers, football was running out of chances to win over a sport-mad, but fickle, local population.

An early Wigan Athletic team photo, date unknown

In the summer of 1900, County were almost immediately replaced by Wigan United. United played in the Lancashire League at Springfield Park for the 1900/01 season, finishing a disappointing second from bottom. But at least senior football was on the menu again in the town and it was seen as important by the powers behind the latest incarnation that apathy for the game had not been allowed to fester.

However, midway through the club's second season, in January 1903, the club saw its lease on Springfield Park expire. With morale and funding now at an all time low, the writing was on the wall and it wasn't long before yet another football team had bitten the dust in the town.

A trend seemed to be developing. It started to look like the people of Wigan just didn't have the stomach to watch a losing team. In the aftermath the question on everybody's lips was would anyone be brave or stupid enough to start another team in the town?

There was no senior football played in Wigan for the next two years until December 1905 when United were superceded by Wigan Town. Were it not for the persistent efforts of a number of dedicated, selfless individuals it is doubtful as to whether football would be being played at the JJB Stadium today.

Scandalously, however, after a promising beginning the 1907/08 season would be the club's last. Lack of funding and local apathy were again blamed. As The Great War loomed the bloodline that had flowed from the first Wigan teams, that would one day breathe life into the Premiership club we know today, was nowhere to be seen.

Come 1919 the people of Wigan were ready to put their support behind a new team – Wigan United (the second team of that name to exist in the town). However, by the 1920/21 season the Lancashire Combination League club had fallen under the spotlight of the Lancashire FA which was questioning its amateur status. The FA demanded that the club turn professional and that the current directors stand down. When the FA was content that United's house was in order the team was renamed Wigan Borough and the penultimate, and perhaps most significant, branch of the Wigan Athletic family tree took shape.

After establishing themselves as an official part-time professional outfit, the non-league club felt they had earned the right to join the hallowed Football League. Thus in a great coup for a relatively young team, Borough were elected to the Third Division North of the League on March 1921. It was a proud day for Borough but also for surviving officials of Wigan County who had set out with the aim of gaining League status as far back as 1897. It was an exciting time for football in the town.

Despite the buzz that the elevation of the team caused, a handful of cynics aired a word of caution. Now the League had accepted Borough into its elite circle the spotlight would be on the town more than ever before. The failure of previous non-league teams in the town was known to have been frowned upon by League members and many had opposed Borough's election. They would watch the club's progress like hawks and any sign of trouble would not only see the club ejected from the league but would likely see Wigan teams ostracised from football's top table for years to come.

Undeterred, Borough became the most organised, professional and established of all the Wigan teams. Though their League adventure would ultimately turn sour they set about it with gusto. Borough played in the town's first Football League game on September 3, 1921, losing in front of an impressive 9,000-strong crowd.

On January 12, 1929 Springfield Park witnessed one of its greatest ever spectacles. A record crowd of 30,443 watched Borough go down valiantly to Sheffield Wednesday in the FA Cup. And so a great FA Cup tradition in the town started. Despite this, the club's finances were imploding. With unpaid players and transfer fees and the growing number of creditors queuing up at the club gates almost outnumbering the fans on the terraces, it didn't look good.

Yet again Borough were a club that was unable to strike a balance between success on the park and financial sustainability off it. The fans' worst fears were realised on October 26, 1931 when directors pulled the plug, forcing the club to withdraw from the League with immediate effect, causing untold disruption.

Directors pulled the plug, forcing the club to withdraw from the league

Astonishingly, with the fall-out from Wigan Borough still crashing down around their ears, plans were already afoot to start a new club. No team would ever have it harder than Wigan's newest. Football fans in the town were as impassive as they'd ever been, the powers that be in the Football League had run out of patience after the Borough debacle and it seemed that after almost 60 years of trying it would take a miracle to establish a lasting senior football team in the town. All in all, it didn't look good for newly formed Wigan Athletic FC.

2   INTO THE CHESHIRE LEAGUE

Wigan Athletic AFC was the sixth senior football club the town had seen in 39 years and none of the previous teams, not County, not United, and not even Borough had as much pressure on them to succeed. You have to admire the sheer determination of those who decided to start a new team in the face of such adversity. It is perhaps that battling spirit, instilled in the club from the start, that would see it through the many trials and tribulations that it would suffer in years to come.

Wigan Athletic, who at the time wore red and white shirts and black shorts and socks, were refused entry to the Cheshire League before making an audacious attempt to join the Football League. With Borough's withdrawal fresh in the minds of the committee, the club was given short shrift. It didn't look good for the Latics. However, an eleventh hour withdrawal from the Cheshire League gave Wigan its chance. A new chapter was about to be written.

Having bought Springfield Park, Charlie Spencer was hired as the club's first manager in August 1932. Spencer was a former England centre-half with League winner's and FA Cup winner's medals to his name. He set about assembling a squad which was peppered with players of League calibre, setting a precedent for the club that would be repeated in future years when the Latics non-league squads were easily good enough to play League football. At the risk of offending, it has always been the 'little' club with big ideas.

The Latics were cementing themselves as one of the top teams in the division

Despite finishing fifth in the league that first season, the club set about overhauling the side for the 1933/34 season. Some questioned Spencer's actions but his wisdom was confirmed when Wigan won the Cheshire League for the first time the following season.

The Latics won the league again the next season and were cementing themselves as one of the top teams in the division. The club also enjoyed unprecedented success in the FA Cup, reaching the third round, thrashing

Charlie Spencer's Cheshire League winning side

Carlisle United 6-1 along the way. It still stands as the record victory of a non-league side over League opposition.

All the efforts of the club's founders seemed to be paying dividends. Crowds were steady and fans were instilled with some confidence that, for the first time, they were putting their support behind a team that would be around for years to come.

In 1936 Wigan won the league for the third time in a row. Spencer's team also won the Cheshire County League Cup and Lancashire Junior Cup to make it an historic treble. Spencer was creating a winning tradition at the club that would see it amass an abundance of silverware in the non-league arena. It was just as well because until the League bigwigs' let the club come in from the cold the fans would have to cling onto any success they could.

The stability and success that Spencer brought to Wigan came to an abrupt end at the tail end of the 1936/37 season. After an eighth place finish in the league Spencer was replaced by Frank Hancock who went on to guide the club to a disappointing eleventh in the league. An air of disgruntlement soon spread across the terraces and crowds began to dip as the mood in the town generally darkened, not least because the nation appeared to be gearing up for another world war. In an ironic way, as Wigan Athletic stumbled along indifferently, the reprieve that the club received by the outbreak of WW2 may have been its saving grace. As the league was suspended, what occupied most fans' thoughts was not how the club would do when the league resumed, but rather whether the club would be there at all.

In the end the club did return to the league after the war. Now though they took to the field for their first game in five years wearing a blue and white strip – a choice forced on them by the fact that it was all the club's impoverished kit supplier could provide. The colours would stick, apart from the odd deviation in the sartorially dubious late 1980s and early 1990s.

That season the Latics finished a disappointing third from bottom. Now they desperately needed a good season to put them back on the Football League committee's radar. However, under manager Jimmy Milne the club faltered again and ended the season rock bottom of the league.

The club appeared listless. After two seasons finishing in the lower reaches of the league a new direction was needed. It was to come when they joined the Lancashire Combination. There are rumours that Wigan had been forced out but, whatever the reason, everyone involved with the club welcomed the opportunity to start afresh in a new league.

Their first season saw striker Billy Lomax join the Latics. Lomax, now 83 and one of the oldest surviving former Latics players, recalls how the 1947/48 season ushered in a new era for the club.

"There was definitely a feeling that it was a new beginning and that money was going to be spent on the team. The crowds were good too. We were getting nearly 6,000 at every game."

The investment in players like Lomax had an immediate effect: come season-end the club topped the Lancashire Combination at the first time of asking. But a mediocre season followed, remembered by fans more than anything else for the sight of England legend Sir Tom Finney turning out for Wigan Athletic in a benefit match. Not everyone enjoyed the winger's performance, however. Billy Lomax, somewhat of a legend himself, has particular memories of the day:

"I didn't enjoy playing with Finney as much as I'd anticipated. At one stage we both broke into the box and he said, 'Here you go, have this goal.' He was only five yards away from me but passed it hard, straight between my legs and I fell over it. I didn't like him for that. Near the end I passed the ball right into his path for an easy tap-in and he missed it completely. I had a little laugh to myself about that."

INCIDENTS FROM THE WIGAN ATHLETIC v. GRIMSBY TOWN FRIENDLY MATCH, AT SPRINGFIELD PARK, WIGAN, MONDAY EVENING, MAY 1st. KICK-OFF 6-30 p.m. ATTENDANCE 16,000. GATE OVER £700.

ATTACK IN THE GRIMSBY GOALMOUTH

1950: Tom Finney played for the Latics in a 5-3 loss to Grimsby in a friendly match

A return to form saw the Latics finish second in the league and almost be rewarded with a surprise election to the Football League in 1950. They just missed out after three polls, however, but the fact that it had required three ballots to eliminate the Lancashire team gave them a glimmer of hope. It had been almost twenty years since Borough had resigned from the League and it now seemed that slowly but surely, attitudes to Wigan Athletic were softening.

In the 1950/51 season the Latics won the league title again. It was the start of a four year spell that would see them finish no worse than fourth. In the 1952/53 season, directors Arthur Horrocks and Sid Littler made funding available for the team to go full-time for the first time. The move saw Ted Goodier's squad storm to the title, also winning a cup treble. Despite this unprecedented success the Latics were still forced to sell their 17-year-old rising star, Les Campbell, midway through the season to pay for the rebuilding of the fire-ravaged Main Stand. Campbell reluctantly moved on but not with the blessing of everyone at the club.

"Arthur Horrocks did not want me to go. He resigned from the board because he didn't think the club should be selling its best players."

Horrocks was eventually persuaded to return to the board, his principles having won him the respect of the fans. He was exactly the type of chairman an ambitious club like Wigan needed as they relentlessly pursued membership of the League. They were applying with virtually every passing season at this juncture. With a couple of other key players following Campbell out the door, Horrocks could never have imagined that the club would top the historic quadruple the following season.

The 1953/54 season was the greatest in Wigan Athletic's early history. After another cup and league clean sweep the Latics went on an heroic FA Cup run which earned them a fairytale third round tie with Newcastle United at St James' Park.

No living person is better qualified than Lomax to sum up the hysteria which hit Wigan in the run up to the match.

"The atmosphere was electric. Wigan had never seen anything like it."

If the atmosphere was good in Wigan you can only image how it must have been in front of the 52,222 that turned out at St James' Park. It was the biggest crowd the Latics' players had ever played in front of but they rose to the occasion.

It was the biggest crowd the Latics' players had ever played in front of

"We felt with the team we had that we should have been there," says Lomax. "When we were 2-1 up we knew we deserved it. That was the first time in my whole career that I'd ever noticed the crowd. After Jackie Millburn equalised I was standing waiting for two minutes for the referee to blow for the restart. I asked him when he was going to blow. 'I've blown it three times!' he said. I couldn't hear him for the crowd."

The 2-2 draw saw the Wigan team crowned heroes. The atmosphere for the replay at Springfield Park was equally electric. Future chairman, Ken Cowap who was on the terraces that day was seduced by the potential as he surveyed the 30,000 strong crowd. The game itself was a fitting spectacle for the occasion even though the Latics lost by the odd goal in five.

The teams come out for the Latics v Newcastle FA Cup Third Round Replay at Springfield Park. 13th January 1954.

Latics v Newcastle FA Cup Third Round Replay at Springfield Park. 13th January 1954.

Into The Cheshire League

*Official programme for the January 1954 FA Cup replay
against Newcastle United*

Lomax is still hailed as a hero in Wigan for his two-goal performance.

"Everyone in Wigan seems to know about that cup run," says Lomax. "Once when I was there I met Dave Whelan. He said to me, 'Today you'd be worth £1 million per week'."

Wigan's FA Cup heroics brought them to the wider attention of the British public and raised their profile with the Football League. At no time in their history had the club a better claim on League status. Alas, it was not to be: the ballot at the League AGM again went against the Latics. Wigan Athletic would have to learn to be patient. Morale amongst spectators and those involved with the club should have been at an all-time high but instead everyone was left wondering just what on earth the club had to do to win favour with the League.

After the club's most successful spell on record Ted Goodier bowed out in 1954 to make way for Walter Crook. He steered the club to a more than respectable third place in the Lancashire Combination but was replaced by Ron Stuart for the 1955/56 season. Stuart was another manager with League experience and the directors hoped it would rub off on the squad. The team was no longer full time, however. When it had been, a couple of seasons earlier, the directors had found it to be an enlightening, but ultimately costly, experiment. One the club was not financially secure enough to repeat.

Though Stuart made a decent start, guiding the Latics to a respectable sixth in the league, he went the way of Crook – the victim of a fidgety board – leaving Billy Cooke and Sam Barkas, in turn, to manage the club in the 1956/57 season as they limped home to tenth place. The managerial merry-go-round was helping no-one and turning the fans against the club. As Dave Whelan found some forty five years later, the club needed a stable platform from which to build for success.

A return to form of sorts took place with the arrival of Trevor Hitchen in 1957. Yet again the manager would only last one season despite steering the team to fourth in the table.

The 1958/59 season marked a nadir for the club. Under the guidance of Malcolm Barrass, and ever so briefly under Jimmy Shirley, the club finished eighteenth in the league. It was a dismal season and it was felt nowhere more than on the terraces where the Latics loyal following was losing patience. The club needed a return to form and quick.

The Latics came out fighting at the start of the 1959/60 season and went on a great run under manager Pat Murphy that would see them finish second in the league. It was not enough to keep Murphy in a job, however, as the board wielded the axe again. Murphy made way for Allenby Shilton.

Shilton's first season saw the club finish third in the Lancashire Combination and in the close season Wigan Athletic sought readmittance to the Cheshire League. At the time there was perceived to be more competition there than in the 'Combi' which, despite their lack of stability off the field, the club had more or less dominated for the previous decade.

Jonny Ball joined as manager for the 1961/62 season. After nine managers in six seasons the fans were crying out for one the board would back. It would be a recurring theme at the club in years to come, right up until the Whelan era. Ball had only limited success at the club. In his first season the Latics finished fifth in the Cheshire League. The 1962/63 season was similarly indifferent. There were problems off the field too. It was rumoured that the fans were paying the players wages some weeks.

Come the following season Allan Brown was hired to spearhead a new drive for admittance to the Football League. Despite his lofty reputation Wigan finished a mediocre twelfth in the league that year. Brown was unfazed. He knew that he was in the midst of a rebuilding job and had already been promised funds to take the team full-time the following season.

Going full-time enabled Brown to attract a far better quality of player to

The 1965/66 Team, 3rd in the League and winners of a cup treble

the club. Les Campbell rejoined and Alfie Craig signed on as captain as Brown steered the cultured side to a first Cheshire League title since 1936 and a cup treble. The team looked unstoppable that year, striker Harry Lyon in particular. Lyon scored a staggering 66 goals to enter club folklore. The feat still prompts older fans at the JJB today to be heard muttering: 'Now Lyon, he was a real striker...'

Brown's team dominated the following season too, winning another cup treble but getting pipped to the league title. Alfie Craig remembers it with great pride:

"We were only beaten nine times over two seasons. One week we were in three cup finals. They used to say at the time that the only thing we never entered was The Grand National. Mind you, with the wingers we had we might have won that too!"

Things were looking up at the club though their outstanding non-league achievements were still not enough to persuade the Football League that they were deserving of a place among the elite. No-one was more frustrated than Brown. After establishing Wigan as the best non-league club in the country he left the club in 1966 to be replaced by Craig. The club would experience yet more success under its former captain with a further cup treble and a runners-up spot in the league. Craig's stay as manager was to be short-lived, however. After clashing with the board he was replaced by Harry Leyland.

Leyland guided the Latics to a disappointing mid-table league finish and fans were starting to question the recent move to the Cheshire League. Still, it would take more than one bad season to dent the club's growing reputation and when plans were hatched to form a new league comprising the top non-league teams from the North of England and the Midlands, Wigan Athletic were one of the first clubs to be invited to sign up. Little did they know when they joined their third league in as many decades that it would be the decisive first step on the ladder to gaining the Football League status that they coveted so badly.

Little did they know it would be the decisive first step to Football League status

3   A FRESH START

The Northern Premier League (NPL) was a fresh start for a lot of ambitious non-league clubs. It was established to mirror the Southern League that Wigan's past FA Cup adversaries Hereford United inhabited. Of the league's 20 founding members, six hailed from the Lancashire Combination (Chorley, Fleetwood, Morecambe, Netherfield, Runcorn, and South Liverpool), six from the Cheshire League (Altrincham, Bangor City, Hyde United, Macclesfield Town, Northwich Victoria, and Wigan Athletic), four from the Midland League (Gainsborough Trinity, Goole Town, Scarborough, and Worksop Town), three from the North Regional League (Ashington, Gateshead, and South Shields) and one from the West Midlands League (Boston United).

The NPL would not only provide increased competition for the top Northern non-league teams who played in it. For Wigan Athletic the real carrot for joining was that it would provide a visible route to the Football League. The NPL, alongside the Southern and Isthmian Leagues, represented the fifth tier of the Football League. Immediately above was Division Four and it was decreed that the NPL winners would be put forward to go head to head in a three-way ballot with their Southern counterparts (from the SPL) and the bottom team from Division Four for a place in the Football League. From there the sky was the limit. It was a huge leap in the right direction for the Latics.

With their eyes firmly on the prize, Wigan Athletic hired former Aberdeen and Leicester player Ian McNeill to lead the team into the exciting new era. McNeill, who would later join Chelsea as assistant manager in an illustrious career, was not the first choice for the post. The board had initially appointed Allan Saunders but just days into the job he was sacked and various rumours circulated.

The new challenge brought about a change at board level too. Local businessman Ken Cowap, who was Wigan born and bred and remained a season ticket holder until his recent death at 80 years of age, was invited to sit on the board. He was to get more than he had bargained on:

"As a fairly prominent Wigan businessman I was approached to go on the board," said Cowap in an interview just days before his death. "I knew Jack Farrimond and Arthur Horrocks already. Sid Littler was chairman at the time.

I went along to my first match as director and sat next to Sid. He said right out of the blue, 'Would you like to buy my shares?' I did, so we shook hands there and then and the deal was done. I recollect that I paid about £5,000 for them."

Though not the wealthiest of owners in the club's history, Cowap was a Latic to the very core and would do anything for the club. Ex-manager and former captain Alfie Craig still regrets that he hadn't managed under Cowap.

"Ken Cowap was the only chairman before Whelan that put any real money into the club. He was as keen as mustard."

Despite Cowap's backing, Ian McNeill had his work cut out to even get a team on the pitch for the club's first game in the NPL.

"When I joined we had about three signed players," says McNeill. "I had to scramble around just to get 11 men on the pitch for that first match. It wasn't easy because there was no money to be spent. Thinking back I don't think I ever paid any real money for a player in all my time at the club."

McNeill used all his resources and contacts in the game to put together a squad littered with players of League calibre. McNeill's great coup was to sign former Manchester United goalkeeper Dave Gaskell. Gaskell played 35 times that first season before being sold on to Wrexham at a profit.

With the club in a new league and boasting an ambitious new owner, the mood on the terraces was buoyant as McNeill led his team out for their first game in the league against Netherfield. As McNeill recalls, it didn't quite go to plan.

"We got beaten by Netherfield who had some players the Latics had released the previous season. After the match I went into the boardroom and one of the directors had a go at me. He started shouting at me: 'F*cking cast offs. We've been licked by a group of cast offs.' I was taken aback and said to him, 'Cast offs? I don't even know these players. It was you that let them go!'"

F*cking cast offs. We've been licked by a group of cast offs

Despite the ominous start, the Latics soon bucked up their ideas and finished their first season in the league in second place. It was a respectable result for the part-time team in a season when Macclesfield ran away with the title.

1969/70

In the close season McNeill strived to bolster his squad. Kenny Morris was one of a group of promising youngsters who came in along with a few seasoned Scottish pros. The club also benefited from arrangements with clubs like Bolton Wanderers who would rather see their players move to Wigan than other League teams where they might come back and haunt them.

The old stadium was starting to look tired in 1969. As the club had struggled through occasional financial crises over the years it had been neglected and was in need of some TLC. McNeill was less sanguine about 'Springy'.

"With no disrespect whatsoever to the club, Springfield Park was a dive. There's no other word for it. On the left side of the ground there was no terracing and what terracing there was, was hopeless. The rain came pouring in through the stand too. It wasn't a great place to watch football and even then you could tell that sooner or later the place needed overhauling or knocking down."

Harold Ashurst, who followed the Latics as a fan but would later join the *Wigan Observer* and become chairman of the supporters club concurs with McNeill.

"I know this might be harsh but anyone who said they had fun at Springfield Park has something wrong with then. It was a dump and it had barely changed since the 1940s. Far from the ground improving over the years it went downhill."

Ian Halliwell, who first knew Springfield Park as a teenage fan but would later become club auditor and owner of favourite Latics' fans 1990s hangout, Rik's Bar, recalls:

"Springfield Park: wild and windy we used to call it. It was the coldest ground in the country. It was a real non-league ground. You could stand where you liked. You could walk up the tunnel, onto the pitch. Nobody would stop you."

To be fair to the club, Ken Cowap was focusing on spending the club's limited resources where it mattered.

"It actually wasn't a bad stadium for the NPL but what money we had went on wages for the team first and then the facilities," says Cowap. "The people of Wigan always wanted a winning team so that was the priority. We were getting crowds of up to 7,000 sometimes then too, so it didn't seem like a priority."

The 1969/70 season was a far sight better than the previous one even if the team could go no better than second place to Macclesfield on goal difference. Better news came in the FA Cup. McNeill's men went on a run bettered only, in terms of media and public interest generated, by the 1953/54 third round tie with Newcastle United.

After seeing off Chorley, Droylsden, Burscough and Skelmersdale, Wigan met League side Port Vale in the FA Cup first round proper. With the first match and replay ending all square the clubs were due to toss a coin to decide the venue for the second replay. McNeill had grander ideas:

"I saw an opportunity so I called Vale's manager and said, 'I think I could get Old Trafford if you fancied it. I'm sure we could take 10,000 fans each'."

Vale's manager agreed and on November 24, 1970 the Latics walked out in front of a 20,000 plus crowd at Old Trafford. 18-year-old Kenny Morris had never experienced anything like it.

"I didn't realise when I went to Wigan that playing for the club would be like that. It felt like a big club for non-league and having someone with League experience and contacts like Ian McNeill really helped us. I remember that we were on £100 a man to beat Port Vale at Old Trafford. Then Freddie Pye and Peter Swales who were at Altrincham but were friends of Ken Cowap came into the dressing room and doubled the bonus. We got £150 for losing! After the match Sir Matt Busby came and commiserated with us. We were all star struck but he was full of praise for us."

Unbeknown to Morris and the other players, McNeill had tentatively arranged to play at Anfield should a further replay have been required. It almost was. Wigan lost only to a freak last minute goal. Despite this, McNeill was removed from his post at the end of the season by the board of directors after having a public disagreement with Horrocks at the club AGM. It threatened the good atmosphere that Kenny Morris recalls had been built up on and off the pitch.

"There was a good team spirit under McNeill. It was a tight knit squad. We spent half the night after training in the Springfield Arms getting p*ssed so we were friends as well as colleagues."

McNeill's departure was a shock to all, not least himself, and Duncan Colquhoun took over as caretaker manager. When news that McNeill's replacement would be former Liverpool player Gordon Milne, fans and players alike started to see that there might be some method to the madness.

1970/71

Milne was just 33 years old when he took up the role of player-manager at Wigan Athletic. Milne played under Bill Shankly at Liverpool where he had won two First Division titles as well as 14 caps for England. He arrived at Springfield Park to great expectation but with a squad still disgruntled at McNeill's departure.

Milne soon won the players over but would never be as popular in his two season spell with the club as McNeill. Milne got the team performing on the park though and with the Latics having finished second in both of the previous seasons there was only one result that would appease the fans.

Luckily for Milne the team got off to a flying start in the Northern Premier League and never really looked back. They won the league by six points from Stafford Rangers, having only lost twice during the whole campaign. Despite the team from that season being remembered as one of the best in Wigan Athletic's history, the young manager had not endeared himself to everyone.

"Milne didn't instil any confidence in the players who hadn't played League football," says Kenny Morris. "He seemed to have a chip on his shoulder about it and definitely had his favourites."

Struggle or not Milne's results speak for themselves. The team also lifted the Lancashire Floodlit Cup, the Northern Premier League Shield and were losing finalists in the Lancashire Challenge Trophy. A run to the third round of the FA Trophy and more significantly a six game run in the FA Cup rounded off a great season. The Latics saw off League opposition in the form of Peterborough Utd in the second round, before succumbing to the European Cup Winners' Cup holders Manchester City 1-0 in the third. Come the end of season the club went to London for the annual League elections even more confident of winning the ballot than they had been in 1954.

Application to the League had been somewhat of a lottery

Application to the League had been somewhat of a lottery for the club before it joined the NPL. Now they knew that as league champions they'd have a one in three chance of being elected. In his ten years on the board, including alternating spells as chairman with Arthur

November 1970: Jack Farrimond, Ian McNeill and the Wigan Team contemplate the FA Cup Replay at Old Trafford against Port Vale. The author's father, Tommy Ross, is pictured front row third from the left.

Horrocks, Ken Cowap dedicated much of his time to trying to finally get the club into the league.

"Ahead of the annual elections I'd spend a lot of time going up and down the country with Jack Farrimond canvassing the League clubs for votes. All the clubs were very nice to us and heard us out. Some promised to vote for Wigan but on the day of reckoning they never did."

Some think that the vote did not go Wigan's way that season due to an ill-advised, but ultimately innocent, publicity stunt. It was not the last questionable stunt that the increasingly frustrated club directors pulled. Cowap was the man responsible for this initial attempt to sway the voters at the Football League AGM.

"We'd topped the league that year so on the advice of a public relations firm I'd hired we got some pens inscribed to hand out to the Football League chairmen. They were Parker pens with 'Wigan Athletic, NPL Champions' inscribed on them. It was common practice to do things like this. Hereford had presented the League with a bull to commemorate the fact they'd won the SPL so the PR firm thought it would be a good idea to put them on the

The 1970/1 team: The author's father is sitting front row, on the right.

Latics v Manchester City (0-1), FA Cup 1971

tables where the Football League chairmen would meet for the vote. The only problem was that they didn't have permission. It didn't go down very well. People thought it was a bribe. It wasn't."

In any case the Latics lost out to Southern Premier League representatives Hereford United at the ballot at London's Café Royal. Cowap and Farrimond felt short-changed. To be fair to Hereford they had taken Newcastle United to a replay in the FA Cup third round with the match televised live on the BBC. It was also the 21st consecutive time that Hereford had come through the preliminary and qualifying rounds of the competition to reach the first round.

Ian Halliwell was not surprised that the Latics did not make it through the hallowed doors of the Football League.

"Though we felt hard done by it seems obvious looking back why the club didn't get in before. At that time we were surrounded by the top clubs like Manchester United, Liverpool, Everton and Manchester City. They were all within a 20 mile radius of Wigan. Then there was Bolton and Blackburn who were still in the lower leagues. Looking back it's madness to consider that the League would let another team from this area enter the League. If you look at the clubs they where choosing over Wigan in those days they all came from towns that had huge catchment areas for fans."

1971/72

In Milne's second and final season in charge the Latics finished third in the NPL. Milne's team did do a cup double, however, lifting the NPL Cup and Lancashire Challenge Trophy. They were runners-up in the Lancashire Floodlit Cup.

The Latics continued their decent FA Cup tradition by making it to the second round before being beaten by Wrexham. The club reached the third round of the FA Trophy too, only to lose to Barnet.

In the minds of Cowap and his fellow directors, Wigan Athletic's claim for a League place was growing. Frustration was setting in due to the constant rebuttal of the League, however. After the failed application the season before someone at the club leaked the story that the Latics were going to seek permission to join the Scottish League after being continually overlooked by its English counterpart. It was nothing more than a publicity stunt but it is said to have drawn the ire of the Football League committee.

Just when it looked like the club had finally shrugged off the stigma of its association with the failed Wigan Borough team, the League had a new grudge to bear against Wigan. It is said that it took three years until the League would even engage with the club following its naïve stunt.

1972/73

Gordon Milne left the Latics in June 1972 to take up a post managing the England Youth team. Les Rigby took over the managerial reins for the 1972/73 season. It was to be another relatively disappointing year. The Latics finished third in the league again, though Rigby's team went on to win the NPL Shield and Lancashire Floodlit Cup. They were also losing finalists in the NPL Cup.

Better news again came in the FA Cup where the Latics drew Lawrie McMenemy's Grimsby Town. McMenemy would later win the competition with a Second Division Southampton side, but his Grimsby side had trouble seeing off the non-league Latics.

"We were all over Grimsby for 90 minutes," recalls midfielder Kenny Morris. "We just couldn't seem to put the ball in the net and eventually conceded a scrappy goal. After the match McMenemy came into the dressing room with the biggest bottle of Champagne we'd ever seen and said, 'Enjoy

Latics head for Wembley for the 1973 FA Trophy Final

this lads. I would have got the sack if you'd won today'."

The Latics also enjoyed a fantastic run to the final of the FA Trophy at Wembley. Conceding just once in eight games, the Latics stepped out against Scarborough, who pipped them to second place in the league that season by one point, with a great chance of lifting the trophy. It wasn't to be and the Latics lost 2-1, to a goal scored four minutes from the end of extra time. Losing late goals in key matches was to become a recurring theme in the club's future.

Ian Halliwell, who had followed the Latics all season

Programme of the 1973 FA Challenge Cup Final

as a 16-year-old wouldn't have missed the trip to Wembley for the world.

"Wigan Athletic was still a family club then. The players were accessible and you felt like you knew them. I thought it would be very different at Wembley but when we arrived and the coach went into the underground car park we got trapped by a police cordon next to the team coach. A friend and I went over and asked the players for their autographs. Kenny Morris said to us, 'Do you want to walk out on the pitch with us lads?' Of course we did. So they walked us through the stadium, up the tunnel and onto the pitch. I'll never forget it. I think they would have let us sit on the bench if we'd asked. It was that type of club."

Halliwell was right. It was a family club but unfortunately it wasn't a very big family. Attendances were down from when the club had first got into the NPL and fans had grown apathetic. Harold Ashurst, who would join the *Wigan Observer* in 1974 covering the Latics, points out that people rarely remember how bad it got.

"We played Darwen and won 11-1 with McLaughlin scoring seven. I thought there were about 3,000 people there but when you look at the records it says there were just 742. Springfield Park was so big it was deceiving but that was a typical crowd in the early 1970s."

In truth the club was treading water financially, with its head only just above the surface. There was growing impatience both on the terraces and in the boardroom with the club's failure to secure League football. The club seemed no nearer to that than when they had joined the NPL full of hope four years earlier.

1973/74

Les Rigby's second and final season in charge was again a relative success. The club finished second in the league just a point adrift of a dominant Boston United. It was a more than respectable result. Rigby's team also lifted the NPL Shield, the Lancashire Challenge Trophy and the Ashworth Trophy to make it a cup treble.

However, the Latics were knocked out in the first rounds of both the FA Cup and the FA Trophy that season, denying the club the money-spinning cup runs they relied on. Incredibly, despite the cup treble and top three finish Rigby would leave the club under a cloud at the end of the season.

It was around this time that Cowap inquired as to whether former footballer and fellow Wigan businessman Dave Whelan would be interested in getting involved at the club.

I knew he was a football man and probably had a bit of money

"I knew Dave from the old days. I knew his father, Jimmy, from the working mens' clubs. I was a magician and a member of the Magic Circle and Whelan's father was a top entertainer in the Wigan clubs. I got to know Dave better from Wigan Market after he'd retired from a football career with Blackburn Rovers. He took over the old ironmongers in Central Chambers on the market square next door to my amusement arcade and turned it into a supermarket.

"As far back as then I'd tried to get him on the board because I knew he was a football man and probably had a bit of money. He came to a board meeting and we explained everything to him but he never took up the offer."

It was a near thing for the club, but at the time Whelan had bigger fish to fry as he made his way in the business world. He would go on to sell his six-supermarket chain of Whelan Discount Stores to Wm Morrison for a reputed £1.5m in 1978. He'd built that business up from owning just one small grocery in Blackburn Market funded by the £400 pay off he received after his promising football career was ended by a broken leg in the 1960 FA Cup final.

In retrospect it probably worked out better for the Latics in the long run. But you never can never tell. With Whelan's business nous and gusto the club might have climbed the leagues long before the late 1990s. Then again, Whelan may never have gone on to make JJB Sports the success that it was which proved such a major factor in later enabling him to spend so much money turning the club's fortunes around.

4   A NEW STAND & NEW IDEAS

The construction of a new 1,300 seater stand at the Shevington End and the addition of a bar and catering facilities with sponsorship from brewers Greenall Whitley gave Springfield Park a much-needed spruce up ahead of the 1974/75 season. The new stand certainly looked the part but it was rarely full enough to pay for its construction.

On the pitch, new manager Brian Tiler brought fresh ideas to the club. A few fresh faces were also brought in to give the team a boost. Not least Tommy Gore who signed from League side Tranmere Rovers and would become a fans' favourite over the next five seasons.

"I was due to go and play in South Africa," says Gore. "Money was an issue because Wigan were part-time in those days. But the manager had contacts in America so he arranged for me to play there in the summer of 1974 before joining up with the squad for pre-season training in July. When I came back to Wigan I had to get a part-time job as a joiner to see me through the season."

Gore returned to the US the following summer to play for Dallas Tornados. He'd play three years without a break after joining Wigan just to make ends meet. During his time with Dallas, Gore played against Pelé in his first game for New York Cosmos.

"I got Pelé's shirt after the game. It was strange coming back to Wigan after experiences like that but I always looked forward to it. I absolutely loved it. We had a really good team in 1974. Increasingly it felt like we were becoming a big fish in a small pond."

Gore's dedication was typical. With the club unable to afford full-time wages all its squad had part-time jobs. The club had learned from experiments in 1952 and 1964 that though having a full-time team always paid dividends on the park – the Latics had won the league in both spells as a full-time outfit – the reality was that if this success was not going to be rewarded with election into the Football League all you would have to show for the investment were a few non-league trophies and a big hole in your bank balance. The club would never, and could not afford to, go full-time again until it gained League status. To even be in with a chance of that they'd need to win the league first. It was a vicious circle.

That is precisely what Tiler's lively team did in his first season there. The

Latics finished four points clear of Runcorn to win the Northern Premier League for the second time. There was no more silverware for the sideboard that season, however. The best the club could muster was a five match FA Cup run before being knocked out by Mansfield Town after a replay and a quarter final loss in the FA Trophy at the hands of Bedford Town.

Wigan Athletic had every reason to believe that they had done enough to be elected to the Football League when directors, Cowap and Horrocks, made the long journey south to the AGM held at the swanky Café Royal in London in early June. However, from past experience the club also had every reason to expect that they would return disappointed to tell those gathered at the Latics social club that it was not to be. In truth the numbers that gathered at the social club to await news were dwindling in proportion to the crowds on the terraces and the annual AGM became a jolly to the capital that Horrocks merely looked forward to for the social aspect.

That day the League were particularly harsh with Cowap and Horrocks. It acknowledged that the club had made great progress on the field but a glance at the club's finances had turned the League off in an instant.

According to one of the League chairmen present that day who asked not to be named, with just over 650 fans attending some home games, the Latics' finances were in a mess. After re-electing Scunthorpe United, who had propped up the Fourth Division at the end of the season, the committee fired out a fierce missive – Wigan Athletic were warned against even applying again to join the Football League until their finances were fully in order.

It didn't come as a surprise to the players. Though their modest wages had always been paid on time and they were largely ignorant to the exact state of the club's finances, some did have an inkling of how hard times were.

"We weren't really aware of there being no money in the club because there was no money anywhere in the league," says Kenny Morris. "Other clubs would sign players for more money than us but if they got knocked out of the FA Cup early there would be a mass exodus because they couldn't afford to pay their wages after Christmas. To their credit Wigan kept paying our wages somehow and honoured our contracts.

"Cowap and Horrocks seemed to finance the club out of their own pockets. Horrocks said to me once, 'If the wife finds out how much I've spent on the Latics she'd go berserk. Cowap was no different. They were both lovely, decent men who were Latics through and through but they just didn't have the big money that you needed to take the club to the next level."

Cowap doesn't dispute the story:

"Yes it cost me a few quid running Wigan Athletic but then running a football club is an expensive hobby. I put lots of money into the club but that's what you're there for. I was born and bred in Wigan and I did what I could for the club. We always managed to get through things and you cannot forget that without the regular and significant help of the supporters club there wouldn't be a club today."

Despite Cowap's, Horrocks', and fellow director Graham Garner's generosity – and the unquantifiable help over the years from the supporters – the club's finances weren't a pretty sight come the summer of 1975. After another season sailing close to the wind it seemed increasingly likely that Wigan Athletic could go the way of Wigan Borough before it.

1975/76

As the purse strings tightened, the club's league form began to suffer. Wigan Athletic finished sixth in the NPL and were knocked out of the FA Cup in the second round by Sheffield Wednesday in the 1975/76 season. The Latics only went one round better in the FA Trophy.

After a trophy-less season the year before, Tiler brought down the curtain on his brief spell at the club with victory in the NPL Shield. It was a respectable return for the money spent on the team and for the number of fans who were coming through the turnstiles but it wasn't enough to save Tiler from the fickle Latics board.

1976/77

Tiler's departure made way for a familiar face to reappear at the club for the 1976/77 season. Ian McNeil's return as manager was as much of a shock to him as his departure had been six years earlier.

"I was manager at Ross County in Scotland and I called Wigan Athletic to see if I could secure a move there for an unsettled player," recalls McNeill. "I expected Arthur Horrocks to answer the phone but Ken Cowap did. He said straight away, 'Ian, would you consider coming back? I never wanted you to go when you did and I'm chairman now.' I said yes, certainly."

As when McNeill had first arrived at the club in 1968 his squad was down to the bare bones. League form was inconsistent and early exits from both the FA Cup and FA Trophy denied the club the money-spinning runs it needed so badly. McNeill must have wondered what he'd done to leave a promising Ross County side for a club who were languishing mid-table with the season barely three months old.

With crowds still hovering around the 1,000 mark at best, newly anointed chairman Cowap and Garner were piling money into the club like never before.

"I'd go to the bank at the end of every week and they'd tell me there wasn't any money for the players' wages," says McNeill. "They'd tell me to go and take it up with Horrocks. He'd always say, 'You better see Ken.' Cowap was a lovely man so I'd go to him reluctantly and ask for the wages. He'd say, 'No problem Ian. Here's the key to my Mercedes, there's bags of shillings and tanners in the boot from the slot machines, use them to pay the players'."

We got paid with the takings from Ken's slot machines more than once

Kenny Morris shares McNeill's memory.

"We got paid with the takings from Ken's amusement arcade slot machines more than once. The boot of his car was always full of coins and had more cash in it than the club bank account."

Garner, remembers another harebrained scheme to keep the club's creditor's from the door. With the country in the grip of a steel shortage wanton gazes had started falling on the imposing Shevington End stand which resembled an unfinished aircraft hangar. The stand was never popular with fans and was a bit of a white elephant for the club. Little did they know that it would save the club from disappearing forever.

"We were skint before we sold the stand. Fortunately a steel fabrication firm agreed to buy it from us," says Garner. "I remember it well. I was watching a match one night and my wife got a message through to me saying we had a buyer for the stand. Boy were we relieved."

The sale of the barn-like construction had indeed saved the club from another sticky situation. To protect the fans from the true state of the club's finances a statement was issued by the Latics saying that the stand was removed because it was too close to the pitch. This was nothing more than a smokescreen.

Noel Ward, who was signed by McNeill from Aberdeen and became a mainstay of the defence confirms that the club certainly wasn't flush with money when he arrived during the 1976/77 season.

"In 1976 McNeill asked me if I would sign for the Latics. I was 22 and I certainly couldn't have lived on the money Ian offered me so it was a bit of a gamble. Of course, it meant finding a full-time job. You have to remember that the club had little or no money in those days. The directors were real gentlemen and genuine Latics fans, but none of them were really wealthy so the manager had to do a lot of wheeling and dealing to get together a decent side."

McNeill did well to assemble a side which combined youthful enthusiasm with Football League experience but the team took a while to gel. The Latics ended the season fourteenth in the NPL. It was their worst ever finish in the league. Cowap was more patient than previous chairman at the club and McNeill was given another season to prove himself. The winning of the Lancashire Junior Cup was scant consolation for the fans who'd seen three managers and numerous players pass through the revolving door at Springfield Park since McNeill's last spell there. A loyal band of fans persisted with the club, however. They could see that the directors were doing everything that they could for the club. McNeill was also seen as a safe pair of hands and the team, which had taken a while to bed in, at last looked like it could really go places the following season.

1977/78

The Latics got off to a blistering start to the 1977/78 season. McNeill's squad was tight knit, worked hard for each other and was probably the best footballing side to have graced Springfield Park since Gordon Milne's day.

The team boasted some genuine talent in the form of Geoff Wright, Joe Corrigan, Tommy Gore and Maurice Whittle and won the Lancashire Junior Cup for the second year in a row. They also reached the third round of the FA Trophy. It was again to be the club's FA Cup form that would bring them to the attention of the nation.

After beating non-league Marine 3-0 in the fourth qualifying round, the

Latics went on to see-off League opposition in the form of York City and Jack Charlton's Sheffield Wednesday in the first and second rounds respectively. Victory over Wednesday was sealed by a memorable Maurice Whittle free kick.

Wigan Athletic's reward for conquering the Yorkshire giants was a plum third round tie with Sir Alf Ramsey's Birmingham City. Ahead of their third round tie against a team boasting one of the rising stars of the day in Trevor Francis, Wigan featured on Granada TV's *Kick Off*. Presenter Gerald Sinstadt and his crew initially wanted to take McNeill's squad to Wembley to film the FA Cup preview special but instead spent the day with the team at a rather decrepit-looking Springfield Park.

Speaking to Sinstadt, McNeill predicted big things for his team.

"The mood is great. The spirit's great and the boys feel we've got a great chance and everybody is bubbling with enthusiasm. Going to Birmingham doesn't worry us at all. We've done one day's extra training, we felt we had to step up a little bit. We beat Stafford on the weekend and had our 19th game without defeat so that'll set us up nicely. Myself and the chairman confidently predict that Wigan will win."

McNeill's confidence and air of cool bred optimism in the dressing room and on the terraces. From groundsman through to chairman, everybody thought the Latics could get a result at Birmingham and the 10,000 fans who traveled south to the game endorsed that belief.

Wigan's player of the year that season, Tommy Gore, recalls with pride how well the team performed.

"We got beat four goals to nil but the only difference between the two teams was Trevor Francis. He had a tremendous game and scored a couple of goals. We played very, very well and Alf Ramsey came into our dressing room after the game and congratulated us. He said he'd expected a more physical game but that we'd played all the football. That meant a lot coming from the man who'd led England to the World Cup a few years earlier."

Alf Ramsey came into our dressing room after the game and congratulated us

Ramsey was indeed impressed with the Latics. He'd expected them to come and kick lumps out of his talented squad. The massive travelling support also reflected well on the club. As Kenny Morris rightly says, "Things really took off for the club then. It really put us on the map."

That was an understatement. Wigan Athletic were in the sports pages of every newspaper and there was a real buzz in the town about the football team for the first time in years. Some even said that if they could top the NPL and just make it into the ballot at the Football League AGM they would have the best chance yet to win the ballot. This was not a view shared by the club or by those fans who had lived through the 34 previous failed Football League applications.

The Latics had got off to a flying start in the league that season but they could do nothing to stop a dominant Boston United team who would agonisingly pip them to the title. It was a massive disappointment, especially considering what was at stake in the bigger picture. Champions Boston United were preparing to fight it out with SPL representatives Bath City and Southport, who had finished bottom of Division Four, for a place in that league when they were informed that their ground did not meet League requirements. As runners up, a completely unprepared Wigan Athletic were given permission to take Boston's place in the ballot.

Almost immediately a buzz went around the town. This enthusiasm was tempered by the old guard of Horrocks and Farrimond who had been down this road many times before. By now, Cowap had sadly resigned his place on the board. But he, as much as anyone, deserved a positive result in London.

Club auditor and fan, Ian Halliwell, remembers that although the optimism among younger fans in the town was not unfounded history counted against the Latics.

"There was no real expectation that Wigan Athletic would get accepted," says Halliwell. "It never once crossed anybody's minds, not least at the club. Saying that, what happened for the first time in 1978 was that the SPL did not put a decent candidate forward. Cambridge, Hereford and Oxford had all got up in previous years. Wimbledon was another good candidate who had got in the year before.

"In the eyes of the League we were still a small northern industrial town with a long list of big clubs in the same catchment area so expectations were still very low. The Football League had always voted for potential, which counted against Wigan."

Nevertheless McNeill and Garner wasted no time in hitting the campaign trail. They travelled the length and breadth of the country canvassing virtually every League club. At that time the First and Second Division clubs got a vote each and the third and fourth Division clubs got six between them. Every vote would count, especially as there were rumours that Southport, who were applying for re-election to the League, had ruffled the feathers of the Football League committee.

Yet *Wigan Observer* sports reporter Harold Ashurst was convinced that the Latics would come home empty handed from the Café Royal.

"I wrote an article on the eve of the vote saying that Wigan Athletic would never get in the League. Arthur Horrocks had said before that the club would get in when no-one expected it to but I don't think anyone really believed that this was the time for it to happen."

Ashurst was probably spot on with his analysis of the situation. On the face of it Wigan could not count on the grace and favour of any of the League chairmen. Unbeknown to the club, however, a higher force was at work. Not the good lord himself but the next best thing: Sir Alf Ramsey was fighting Wigan Athletic's corner.

McNeill had travelled down to witness the vote with Farrimond, Garner and Horrocks and remembers it like it was yesterday.

"It was very tense and we didn't really have high expectations to be honest, despite all the canvassing we'd done. In the first vote Southport and Wigan got 26 votes each and Bath City who were non-league like us got 18 votes. It was a great result and there was a bit of confusion before it was announced that there was to be a re-vote between Southport and Wigan."

Recording the same number of votes as the League club was a watershed for Wigan. It had never been this close to being elected before. And it had England's World Cup winning manager to thank. After being impressed with the club and its fans during the FA Cup third round tie with his Birmingham side, Ramsey had taken a liking to the club. When the Latics received a shock call-up for election to the Football League that summer he is thought to have immediately asked fellow Midland clubs Aston Villa, Wolverhampton Wanderers and West Bromwich Albion to vote for the Lancashire club. Though the exact apportioning of the vote was never released it is thought that this powerful block of votes enabled the Latics to tie with Southport in the first ballot.

McNeill. who was left pacing the corridor as the second vote commenced, was optimistic.

"I didn't need to watch the next vote because once Bath City were eliminated I knew we'd get most of their votes because they were non-league like Wigan. I'll never forget when the door opened and this small, officious man strode out with a puffed up chest and said, 'Wigan's in!' I later learned that Ramsey was great to us, which was an amazing gesture from a man like him. You could say that he's partly responsible for where Wigan are today. I can't describe how good it felt to get into the League and how happy I was for the club and everyone who had chipped in to keep it going over the years. It was great for the fans that had stuck by us too. However high Wigan would eventually go in the League, that was the first step."

After 34 failed attempts and against all the odds, Wigan Athletic were elected into Division Four of the Football League by a margin of nine votes. League football was to return to Wigan after a 47 year hiatus since Wigan Borough's collapse. Back in the town, news had filtered through of the shock result and the social club was filling up with disbelieving fans as the party got into full swing. Echoing what it meant to the town, McNeill's neighbours hung a big sign saying 'Well Done!' across the street.

Ian Halliwell was as surprised as anyone:

"It was a complete and utter shock. The club hadn't anticipated it, and it certainly wasn't geared for it. I was sitting in my office at Bartons Accountants in Wigan that afternoon and club secretary Derek Welsby called me. Derek was a small, unassuming chap who never swore so when he did I knew something big had happened. He said, 'We're bloody well in Ian. I don't know how but we're bloody well in. I'll be in to see you on Monday,' he said, 'We've got to do budgets and get the accounts in order for the League'. Derek wanted to do it properly."

The Wigan delegation left London that sunny afternoon on June 2, 1978, feeling like they were walking on air. When they eventually got back to Wigan the party was still raging and they got a heroes reception. McNeill remembers that it was a struggle to drag Horrocks away from the bright lights of the Capital.

"Arthur wanted to stay in London and go out on the town to celebrate but as I was driving I said, 'No way. You stay if you want. I'm going back to Wigan. There's a lot of work to do tomorrow'."

Never had a truer word been spoken.

5   FORWARD TO THE LEAGUE

The people of Wigan woke with a collective hangover on June 3, 1978. The pain was immediately eased by the realisation that the club had League football to look forward to for the first time in its 46 year history.

Club officials woke to the same realisation but also to the stark reality that the club had a lot of hard work ahead to even make it to the centre circle on the first day of the 1978/79 season. No two people would work harder to get the club in order than secretary Derek Welsby and auditor Ian Halliwell who was hired to bring the Latics' financial house into order. Unless that could be done before the start of the season the Latic's place in Division Four would be in severe jeopardy.

Halliwell is one of the few people alive who was party to what went on behind the scenes during those frantic summer months. His detailed account of the process makes compelling reading.

"I became the club accountant in 1977. It was the first time they'd appointed auditors. I got the job on the basis that I was the only one in the firm that followed football. My boss said, 'You know football, you do this one'.

"Welsby wanted to bring the club into some sort of administrative well-being. The way the club was run then was amazing. None of the directors were loaded and there wasn't a great deal of money in the club. They only got involved for the status.

"After receiving the news from London on Friday, Welsby had called me to say that he wanted to do budgets for the season and get the accounts in order for the League. Welsby wanted to do it properly. On the Saturday I was playing cricket and he turned up in a panic. He had some documentation from the Football League which needed filling in and he didn't know where to start. I went down to Springfield Park the next day and not a lot of people know this but Wigan Athletic's League adventure was almost over before it had even began.

"The club was totally amateurish. It was a shambles. Those were the days when there were no electronic turnstiles, there were no computers or calculators. It was expected that the guy on the turnstile got his cut and that the supervisor skimmed off his cut too. Budgets didn't exist. In the past if they'd wanted a player, one of the directors would cough up £250. It was all done out of the back pocket. It was typical non-league.

"Point one of the Football League form asked for the details of all the club's shareholders. According to the official ledger which dated back to the early 1930s the shareholding of the club in 1978 comprised 15,000 ordinary £1 shares. The year before as part of the audit I had already contacted Companies House to compare the list of shareholders that they had with the ledger at the club. Of the 15,000 shares we could only verify the ownership of 6,000, which was a minority stake in the club, held by the directors and about 30 smaller shareholders from the town. Over 8,000 of the club's shares belonged to people from Wigan who'd subscribed to them in the 1930s.

We couldn't account for over half the club's shareholders

"This was a massive problem. How could we tell the League that we couldn't account for over half the club's shareholders? So we cut some corners and we wrote to everybody we could saying that if we didn't hear from them in ten days we'd consider that they were no longer living and able to claim ownership of the shares. We moved heaven and earth in the month that we had to submit everything. We got people out knocking on doors to make every effort to find the missing shareholders.

"Eventually we did account for another 500 shares and we decided to split the outstanding 8,500 shares proportionally among the other shareholders. Without doing that Wigan Athletic would not have even got over the threshold into the League."

The fun was only just beginning. Ian McNeill didn't even have a full team. The players he had, had signed up for another part-time season in the Northern Premier League before going on holiday. In a day before mobile phones, faxes and emails it was easier said than done to track the squad down. According to Halliwell the job fell to Welsby:

"Half of the players were on holiday at that time but Derek said he'd try and track them all down. He had to do it the hard way. It was chaos, but within a fortnight he'd rounded most of them up and we were ready to start contract negotiations.

"I attended a board meeting the Tuesday after they'd been voted into the League and suddenly the club was faced with a whole new proposition. Apart from McNeill and Welsby, everybody else at the club was part-time. Overnight they were required to become a professional club.

"At the meeting, Horrocks asked McNeill if he needed any more players. McNeill said, 'More players? We don't even have a team! Some of these players will not leave their day jobs to turn professional'. The chairman couldn't understand that there were players who would earn more staying in their day jobs than playing full time football. We had some well-educated boys in the team with good careers. For example, Jonny King and Jonny Rogers had already told the club that it couldn't afford to match what they earned as it stood."

Luckily for McNeill, for every player who refused to turn professional, there was one who would have taken anything the board offered just to play League football.

"Most of the players decided to go full-time without the bat of an eyelid," says McNeill. "Most of them lost money by giving up their day jobs so I told them if they had a good year I'd make it up to them. They were all just desperate to play. That was what I liked about that team."

Tommy Gore was one of the squad that leapt at the opportunity regardless of the salary on offer.

"We mostly all went full time when we got into the League. Everyone was worse off financially. Most of us got £75 per week during the season and £60 in the summer."

In truth, the salary negotiations were a complete shambles.

"After losing Rogers and King the board had panicked and were offering the players whatever they asked for," recalls Halliwell. "Nobody at the club knew what the average Fourth Division player earned. They had no budget drawn up. I was sitting in the corner of the room totalling the figures up after the board had negotiated with each player. After nine players I saw that there was no control over what was being spent.

I saw that there was no control over what was being spent

"Ian Gillibrand was our first captain in the League. He did not expect to be offered a contract because of his age and would have done anything to have just one season in the League. Before he came in to see the board Horrocks said, 'We can't afford to lose Ian.

Let's give him what he wants'. They offered him about £120 per week, and Ian couldn't believe it. He would have accepted half that."

Halliwell watched on in disbelief as the same thing happened over and over again until McNeill came in to discuss his new package. By then the penny had dropped with the board that they were paying far too much to the players. McNeill didn't get anywhere near the contract he wanted. There was no more money left for coaches Kenny Banks and Duncan Colquhoun either. Worse was to come according to Halliwell.

"The one person they'd bypassed completely was Derek. He turned to me and said, 'Ian, they've not discussed my wages!' This was after him tracking down the players from all round the country and writing all the contracts. The one thing they would not spend money on was back office staff and support staff for the manager.

"When they'd spoken to all the players and coaching staff, Horrocks said, 'How much is our weekly wage bill?' When I told him he almost choked 'We don't take that f*cking much on the gate!' I knew there was no way the club could afford it. Based on the contracts we'd offered the players, some of which were four years long, Derek said to me that by the time those contracts expired the current board would be history."

It was a real gamble and only time would tell if it would pay off. The board's expectation was that Wigan Athletic were back in the League to stay. Horrocks arrogantly presumed that the club would walk the Fourth Division. In the previous decade clubs such as Cambridge, Hereford, Oxford and Wimbledon had got into the League and shot right up a division straight away. The Wigan board naively thought that the club would do the same.

After much scrambling around behind the scenes by Halliwell and Welsby, Wigan Athletic somehow satisfied the League that they were in good enough fiscal shape to take their place among its members. The team stepped out proudly on August 19, 1978 for their first League fixture, away to old non-league foes Hereford Utd. The nil-nil draw satisfied McNeill but the Latics would take only three points from their next six games. Their next game, and first home game in the league, was against Grimsby Town on August 23. A crowd of 9,227 turned out to see the home side well-beaten 3-0. The size of the crowd, if not the result, was a positive but only if it could be sustained. The club did not register its first League goal until September 2, 1978 when Joe Hinnegan scored in a 2-3 loss to Newport County. The Latics would have to wait until September 13 to record their first league win, a 3-0 victory against Rochdale.

The one ray of light in that difficult few weeks was a 2-1 victory over Tranmere Rovers in the League Cup when Frank Corrigan became the first Latics player to score a goal in the competition. The Latics bowed out of the cup soon after at the hands of Luton Town.

Tommy Gore remembers how hard some of the squad found the transition from non-league to League football.

"The football was a big step up but having only got admitted to the league in June it was a rush to get the squad

A programe from Wigan's first match in the League

ready for the start of the season. The main thing I remember was the difference in training full time compared to playing part time and working. We'd only been doing full time training for six weeks and it was draining because it was so new to us.

"After the season had been underway for a month or so it got better. We were playing two games a week so we didn't need to train so hard and could vary it. The loss to Grimsby was a reality check for everyone though. They beat us comfortably but after a few weeks we were fully acclimatised and went on a bit of a run."

Gore is being modest. It got a lot better. After the club had sunk to third bottom in the table, the Latics went on a seven game unbeaten run to climb to seventh, just three points off third place. Things kept improving after this run, as player of the year Gore recalls:

"Once we'd played everyone once our confidence grew and we knew that we had the beating of most of the teams. You have to remember that we all had something to prove in the League too. Everyone thought they could play at that level."

Centre back Noel Ward, whose consistent form would earn a call up to the Northern Ireland squad, remembers how the crowds starting coming back to Springfield Park with the promise not just of League football but of winning football.

"We pulled ourselves together as the season went on and started climbing the table. We got the crowd up from a few hundred in the non-league days to a few thousand every week."

Despite more people coming through the turnstiles it seemed like the Latics fans would never be happy. One game sticks in McNeill's mind from that season that demonstrated how fickle and impatient some of the support could be.

"We played Port Vale at home that season. It was on Friday the 13th of April, 1979, ironically. We were losing three nil at half time and a guy jumped down from the terrace and threw his season ticket at me. He said, 'McNeill, stick it up your arse!' I made some changes at half time and we ended up winning 5-3 to go fifth in the league. You'd think we were fifth bottom from his reaction.

"The next day I said to Derek, 'You'll be getting a call from someone saying they've lost their season ticket, put them through to me please'. Later on that day my phone rang and it was a lady on the other end. She said, 'Mr McNeill, my husband lost his season ticket at the match. I said, 'Ah, yes. Well, your husband gave me his season ticket on Friday and told me to put it somewhere. Tell him I did and I can't get it back out!'"

All in all the Latics first season in the League was a success. After a shaky start the club lost only seven out of the last 30 games to end the season in sixth place, ten points behind winners Reading. It was a good start in the Fourth Division but one that could have promised so much more.

"We finished sixth but if we'd only got a few more points in the first games we would have got promotion that first season," says McNeill. "I'm positive of it."

Off the field the club's shaky finances began to cause concern, especially in light of the fact that the club had not been promoted as some had expected. As the season wore on it became obvious that Halliwell's fears were being realised.

"There were no systems in place, no control over money that first year," says Halliwell. "The directors had no inclination of what was happening. They assumed that they were going to get promoted. They assumed that the crowds were going to go up from the 9,000 they'd got at the first home match of the season when in reality we'd be lucky to sustain half that. They assumed that the club could be self-financing.

"When they didn't go up straight away the cracks began to appear. The bad practices of the non-league were continuing too. I remember going to matches and the announcer would say that there were 5,000 people there. I'd look around and it would be clear that there were 7,000. I knew that it was all cash on the gate and no tickets or paperwork. They'd just come in with a bag of cash and pour it onto the table. This lasted all the way up to 1980/81. All the wages were paid in cash too. The chairman would sometimes go into the dressing room with a bunch of fivers and say, 'You can split that if you win today'.

"On the plus side they were getting regular crowds of 5,000 that first season, which was an improvement on the non-league days, but nothing changed. The massive debts that were amassed in those fledgling League years can be put down to the amateur way in which the directors ran the club. They were all great guys, passionate about the club but they just didn't have the nous or the money to run it properly. It's a miracle that it survived at all in those days."

A major contributing factor to the financial state of the club

They just didn't have the nous or the money to run it properly

was Farrimond's and Horrocks' belief that the club were going to get crowds of 12,000 a week and ride up through the divisions on the wave of cash. In reality it was never going to happen. In those days the rugby league club, which still dominated the sporting landscape in the town, were only getting crowds of 10,000.

"Jack and Arthur could not grasp that this was still a rugby town at heart and that they needed a plan of how to grow the support like the club has done under Whelan," says Halliwell. "Instead they did everything on impulse. They'd buy players and sack managers on a whim with no real regard for where the club was heading."

Where the club was heading was to the wall. At the rate it was going it wouldn't be long before the club was back where it had come from.

1979/80

In the close season McNeill strengthened the Latics squad bringing in, amongst others, a certain young Michael Quinn from Derby County. Mickey Quinn, he of 'Who ate all the pies' and 'He's fat, he's round, he's worth a million pound' fame, was a hungry young striker when he joined the club. Quinn joined a large group of Scousers at the club including Tommy Gore and settled in straight away.

Soon after Quinn joined, McNeill received a telephone call at Springfield Park.

"Quinn had been at the club a few weeks when my telephone rang," recounts McNeill. "It was someone from the DHSS. They said, 'Do you have a Michael Quinn playing for you?'

I said, 'Yes, I do.'

'Are you paying him?'

'Yes, of-course, he's on contract with us.'

'Oh. It appears that Mickey is also claiming unemployment benefit back in Liverpool'."

McNeill called Quinn into his office the next day but could barely keep a straight face when he told him what had happened. Quinn, who'd been afraid of how McNeill might react was relieved to be told, 'I won't tell the chairman if you go out and score some goals for me this season'.

That season we started getting bigger crowds than the rugby

To the relief of the club the fans flooded back to the terraces when the 1979/80 season began. Still, even with several thousand in Springfield Park it never felt full.

"That season we often got bigger crowds than the rugby," says Gore. "We were getting 6,000 but the stands were a long way from the goals so people tended to congregate at the sides. It's safe to say that no team liked visiting Springfield Park."

The Latics didn't always exploit home advantage, however, and were knocked out of the League Cup in the first round by Stockport at home before the league had even got underway. Wigan's first league match that season saw them draw 2-2 away to Darlington. Their first home game saw them lose to Huddersfield Town after which the club lost six of the next ten. It left the Latics languishing in nineteenth place in the table. It wasn't the start the club would have wished for as it targeted promotion.

The Latics form improved from there and they won four of the next six matches. The short run of form left the club in an improved thirteenth position on the eve of its FA Cup first round tie with Blackpool. McNeill's team drew 1-1 in the seaside town, going on to win by two goals to nil in the replay. This would be the start of a cup run that would see Wigan Athletic's name gracing the back pages of national newspapers once more.

Before its second round meeting with non-league Northwich Victoria in the FA Cup on January 5, 1980, Wigan enjoyed a five game unbeaten run in the league enabling it to climb up to eighth in Division Four. It took a replay to see off

Latics took thousands of fans to West London to tackle the mighty Chelsea

plucky Northwich Victoria but the Latics were rewarded with a dream third round tie against Chelsea at Stamford Bridge. Cup fever returned to the town once more and the Latics took thousands of fans to West London to tackle the mighty Chelsea.

Tommy Gore starred for the team that day.

"I'll never forget that game at Chelsea because I scored the winner. It was a great result because they were top of the second division after a spell out of the top flight and had Geoff Hurst as manager and some big names on the pitch. It was also the only FA Cup match played in London that day because of the bad weather, so it got a lot of media coverage. That was the first time after being elected into the league that we put ourselves on the map."

A contributing factor to Wigan Athetic's victory that day was the footwear that McNeill had provided to help his team cope with the frozen pitch. That was the day the club played its part in helping send small sportswear manufacturer Reebok on its way to becoming a global brand.

"You could say I played a major part in the establishment of Reebok," says

McNeill with a wry smile. "I played golf with a chap who had a local sportswear company. We were talking about playing football in the frost and he said he had a boot that had bars and round suckers that gave you more grip than normal boots. We used them against Chelsea and won 1-0 with Tommy Gore scoring a cracking goal from 30 yards.

"After the match I was interviewed on television and I thought I'd give the company a little boost so I said, 'It just goes to show, you don't need to use this foreign Adidas rubbish'. There was quite an uproar. An Adidas rep called to ask me what I thought I was doing."

The Latics' reward for conquering Chelsea was a plum away tie to First Division Everton. Sadly the Lancashire club couldn't overcome the Merseysiders to make it to the fifth round for the first time, though the experience of playing in front of 53,000 at Goodison Park, with an estimated 20,000 from Wigan, is one that few of the players will ever forget. The 3-0 scoreline will be easier to erase from the memory.

Off the park too, the company the club was keeping seemed to have gone up a notch. McNeill's wife Sheila recalls:

"At the game at Goodison I was in the executive lounge and one of the directors heard I was from Aberdeen. He said he had a shop up there. I was wracking my brains to figure out what this little store could be and I asked him what it was called. 'Littlewoods', he said!"

The FA Cup run proved that Wigan could cut it with the big boys

The FA Cup run had given the club a boost in confidence which spilled over into the league. The Latics lost just three times in the final 22 games to end the season in sixth place. It was frustrating for the players because the FA Cup run proved that Wigan could cut it with the big boys. With every cup run – and there would be several over the next few seasons – the club's hunger for promotion stiffened. But yet again the team's promotion aspirations had been undone by a poor start to the season.

"People got frustrated when we'd been in the league for a couple of years and hadn't been promoted," recalls Gore. "The fans wanted more."

The practice of banking on promotion to balance the books also took its toll as the season ended. Farrimond and Horrocks had done their best for the club, even upgrading the stadium that season, but it was time for the Latics to enter a new era as a professionally run club. The non-league practices needed to be left behind for ever. As Welsby had predicted just a couple of years before, the time had come for change.

"When they didn't go up the first two seasons the damage was done for the board," says Halliwell. "A new board had to come in. It was just a matter of who rather than when."

6   BOARDROOM MANOEUVRES

Exactly who would move into the boardroom at Springfield Park would be resolved sooner than anyone expected. The club's newly elevated status, modest underachievement and poor financial state, were causing a few vultures to start circling. The chairman of one of Wigan Athletic's former non-league adversaries was taking a particularly keen interest.

McNeill was given a final chance to win promotion for the Latics in the 1980/81 season. Behind the scenes massive changes were already afoot. Ken Cowap, who had stepped down from the board some four years earlier, was to receive a surprise windfall for his club shares.

"I got a phone call out of the blue from Freddie Pye asking me if I wanted to sell my shares. I'd forgotten all about them. They were valueless as far as I was concerned but I decided to sell. It was a good offer and I made my money back and Pye said he'd put some money into the club to get it out of the division which was what the club needed."

It was to be a fresh start for the club. Pye, who had been manager at Altrincham saw massive potential. His arrival saw Horrocks promoted to president of the club. It was a well-deserved title for a dignified, honourable gentlemen who had done his best for the club.

The players, fans and not least McNeill had no idea what to expect from the new chairman.

"One of the first times I'd met Pye was when we were playing Altrincham away from home. One of our players scored and came running over to the bench to celebrate. Pye got up out of his seat, picked up the trainer's sponge bucket and threw water all over the scorer. I wasn't sure what was in store for the club."

Things got off to a decent start for the Latics. They dispatched Crewe Alexandria over two legs in the first round of the League Cup but opened their 1980/81 league campaign with two losses on the trot. A loss to Preston in the second round, first leg of the League Cup made it three in a row. McNeill was under pressure with the season barely a week old.

Despite having a new chairman at the helm, money was still tight. It was already rumoured that Pye was going to bring in his own manager and McNeill certainly wasn't given big money to spend on the threadbare squad.

Current club physio Alex Cribley was one new face that McNeill brought in during September 1980. Centre back Cribley was surprised at the lack of resources available to the club.

"Despite being established in the Fourth Division, money was tight, facilities were tight, kit was even tight. We used the terraces for training and practised on a council pitch next to the stadium. There was no training kit to speak of. It was a case of first up, best dressed. If you were in early you got the little kit there was. If not you used your own or got the ragged stuff that was full of holes. I drove in from Liverpool with some of the other lads. We were always last there so got the dregs. The spirit was good though."

The team would need that spirit in spades as it went on a run that left it in the bottom third of the table at Christmas. There wasn't much festive cheer for the fans and discord soon spread from the terraces to the dressing room in the New Year. Despite two back to back home wins in early February, which came after a five match spell where the club had lost three times, the writing was on the wall. The club were receiving letters and returned season tickets from fans and there were sporadic 'McNeill out' chants on the terraces.

Sitting tenth, Wigan's home match against second from bottom Port Vale on Valentine's Day took on a make or break complexion for McNeill. Such is the way in football. The Latics played dismally, losing 3-0. McNeill's time at the club was over, save for the briefest of returns in the Dave Whelan era, and Fred Eyre was installed as caretaker manager.

McNeill went down to the club on February 16, 1981 to bid farewell to his squad. He'd always enjoyed a good relationship with his players. He'd enjoyed a more fractious relationship with the board, especially that season. McNeill acknowledged that his time at the club was coming to an end when the board started interfering with football matters.

"Towards the end of my time there, Pye called me one day to say that he was going to take Bobby Charlton onto the board," says McNeill. "A few days later Charlton came and asked if he could help with the training. I wasn't happy with it but he was a director so I told him to please himself.

"He came and took the midfield players for a walk round the training ground. Then he left and the players rejoined us. I said to George Urquart, 'Was it enlightening?' He said, 'Enlightening? Charlton said, 'At Manchester United George Best used to do this and I'd do that....' I told him if I could do what Best does I wouldn't be at Wigan Athletic!"

Caretaker manager Eyre took charge of his first game for the Latics at home to top three club Mansfield Town. The Latics won 2-0. Eyre's second game in charge saw the team draw 0-0 away to Bury. A draw was seen as a good result in light of what had happened on the coach on the way to the game. Eyre and his players learnt from a radio bulletin that former Nottingham Forest and England defender Larry Lloyd had been appointed player-manager. It was news to all of them and bred contempt for the board with Eyre and his squad. If the players thought they'd feel more at ease after meeting the imposing 6' 3" Lloyd they were sadly mistaken.

Lloyd's reign at the club started in a brutal manner. With the players

If you don't like what I'm going to say then I'm going to head-butt you

waiting to meet him for the first time, expecting to hear the usual line that they'd all get a chance to prove themselves, Lloyd burst through the door. As Mickey Quinn recalls:

"Larry slammed the door open, nearly taking it off its hinges, strode in and bellowed, 'Hello I'm Larry Lloyd. If you don't like what I'm going to say then I'm going to head-butt you'."

With the club sitting tenth in the table, Lloyd, who became renowned for his uncompromising managerial style, had ten games to turn the club's fortunes around. It wasn't to happen. After three losses, two draws and two wins from the next seven, the Latics dropped to eleventh position where they'd remain for the rest of the campaign.

1981/82

After a season of turmoil a new dawn had broken at Springfield Park. There was a new sheriff in town and he was going to drag the club by the scruff of the neck toward the top of the table whether the players and fans liked his methods or not.

Lloyd arrived in Wigan with only his reputation bigger than his imposing physical presence. A two-time European Cup winner with Brian Clough's Nottingham Forest, Lloyd was brought in with the express aim of taking the team up a division. Crucially, Freddie Pye was going to give Lloyd the financial backing to do it.

Alex Cribley remembers a lot of new faces arriving at the club and the immediate impact it had.

"Pye made a lot of money available to Larry and that was the start of the club's climb really. Lloyd was given cash to bring in players like Graham Barrow and Clive Evans. I remember that we scored a lot of goals from set pieces that season which made a big difference. We had some big players in the side like Colin Methven and Larry himself."

Lloyd overhauled what remained of McNeill's squad but it didn't enable the club to get off to a winning start in the league. The Latics drew its first game against Bradford City and lost its following two league matches. Better form came in the League Cup with the club beating fellow Fourth Division team Stockport County 5-1 on aggregate. That win on September 14 saw the club start a seven match unbeaten run in the league.

By October 17 they were eighth in the table, just four points off second. A 5-3 loss to Bury dampened the mood but Lloyd's well-drilled unit would not lose in the league again until March 16, 1982. In fact, in cup and league the club lost only twice in the next 26 games, one of those a 2-1 defeat at the hands of Aston Villa in the fourth round of the League Cup. The Latics had beaten Chelsea 4-2 at home prior to that.

Wigan's impressive run during the early months of 1982 saw them hit top spot in Division Four on January 26. The club would only lose seven times in the league all season on the road to promotion. A 3-1 home win against Mansfield Town secured the club's first promotion in the Football League. They could have been champions that year, and probably would have deserved it. Going into the last match of the season against sixteenth placed Aldershot, the club were just two points off first place. The Latics couldn't avoid a 2-0 home defeat that saw them slip to third, however.

The success of Lloyd's team brought the fans back to Springfield Park that season, as Cribley recalls:

"The year we went up we did get good crowds. We were getting 10,000, sometimes even 15,000 when we were playing the top teams like Sheffield United. You'd look at it and think it really could take off if the fans kept coming every week instead of just for the big games."

The fans may have been happy but Lloyd didn't endear himself to all the players during their promotion-chasing season. Mickey Quinn, no featherweight himself, recalls going toe to toe with Lloyd a few times as tempers got frayed. Once Lloyd even told Quinn and namesake Tony Quinn not to come back out after halftime after a dismal first half performance, only to realise that with just one substitute to use, the team would have to play with ten. Mickey Quinn was summoned from the bath and given a reprieve but it would be the beginning of the end of his time at the club. Graham Barrow too almost came to blows with Lloyd on the training ground on more than one occasion.

Whether Lloyd relished the confrontation is uncertain. However, his results cannot be argued with. What is clear is that the Lloyd era ushered in a new age of professionalism at the club. It was no longer as accessible to the fans as when McNeill had been there. McNeill would happily drink with the fans in the social club and encourage players to do the same. Lloyd had come directly from playing at the highest level where players have to be distanced from fans for their own protection. He brought some of that aloofness to Wigan Athletic.

Another thing which also made the fans feel that the club as they knew it had gone forever was when Freddie Pye brought a group of new directors onto the board in the face of reported £250,000 debts. Harold Ashurst, who covered events at the club for the *Wigan Observer* at the time, remembers the uproar it caused.

"Pye spent a lot of money getting the club promoted so he brought Ken Bates, Fred Summers and Eric Barnes onto the board. They, along with Pye and Charlton, were known as the Manchester Mafia. They were Manchester businessmen and seemed to have no feeling for the club whatsoever. Bates was said to have bought quite a big stake in the club and nobody understood why he got involved. He seemed to have no ambition for the club and didn't stay for long. You could ask that of any number of chairmen from the 1980s."

1982/83

Despite winning promotion for the Latics and bringing cult figures to the club like Graham Barrow, Colin Methven, Kevin Langley and Eamonn O'Keefe, who was a club record signing in January 1982 for £65,000, Lloyd wouldn't see out his second season.

The club's debt would be a big factor. Not only had a huge amount of money been spent on the park to bring the club up a league. Off the park the club had also ambitiously spent money, some of it raised by the supporter's

Larry Lloyd and the Squad, 1982-83

club admittedly, to provide increased covered seating and to build a new executive suite for the directors. Quite what the fans thought of the club spending money so the directors could watch in more comfort when the club had spiralling debts is anyone's guess. To the delight of those on the terraces the 'Golden Jubilee Executive Suite' had such poor ventilation that visiting bigwigs had to continually wipe away the condensation just to keep up with the action.

An uncorroborated story from someone involved with the club at the time also implies that the Latics financial woes weren't helped by picking up the tab for one of the new directors to go to watch the 1982 World Cup in Spain. Their expenses were said to be 'astronomical'.

Alex Cribley remembers that there was an immediate pinch that first season in Division Three.

"The cost of going up caused a lot of problems and it cost Larry his job. There was simply no more money for it to push on from there."

Ominously, Wigan Athletic bowed out of the FA Cup in the first round and the League Cup in the second in the 1982/83 season. It was always going to be tough playing in a higher league, especially with the minute budget Lloyd was given to bring in better players, but the Latics made a real go of it early in the season. In the first ten Division Three matches the club won and lost five apiece. The club sat in twelfth place, exactly mid table and had scored 23 goals in that spell so were at least providing the fans with some entertainment.

The 4-0 loss away to Bristol Rovers on October 16, 1982, started a run of six league games without a win. The one point they earned in that time could not stop the club slipping to seventeenth. The pattern for the season was set. After eleven matches without a win in the New Year, Lloyd's team still inhabited seventeenth place and some Latics fans were proving again that they didn't have the stomach to watch a losing team. Ironically, it was precisely the time when directors were counting on every penny taken on the turnstile.

The pressure on Lloyd was mounting from the board who demanded better. The 3-1 win against Wrexham on April 4, which saw the club climb one place in the league, was not enough to save him, however. After a furious row with the board, Lloyd was sacked by Pye to be replaced by Bobby Charlton. Lloyd's place in history was secured, however. He will be remembered for a long time to-come as the man who first won the club promotion in the League.

Charlton would look after first team affairs for much of the rest of the season until Lloyd's successor, Harry McNally, was appointed. Current reserve/youth team coach David Lowe, who was an up and coming star for the Latics at the time, remembers the stir it caused when the World Cup winner took over the team affairs.

"Charlton joined in at training and was the best player there by far. Before matches he used to give us a hot toddy before we went out. It was different to what we were used to."

Without Lloyd the team fared well in the run in. In eight matches the Latics lost just three times. The club ended the season in a disappointing eighteenth place, however. Bearing in mind the importance of consolidating in a new league, the Latics 2005/06 debut Premiership season being a good example, it wasn't a terrible result.

Funding problems off the park, not helped by Ken Bates' departure for Chelsea, were, however, slowly ripping the heart out of the club. With the greatest respect to Pye, it is safe to say that the club's finances imploded and as the team walked out for its end of season tie with Preston it was mooted that, with the club running on fumes, it could have been the last in the club's 50 year history. Ex-player and manager, the late Jimmy Shirley, is credited

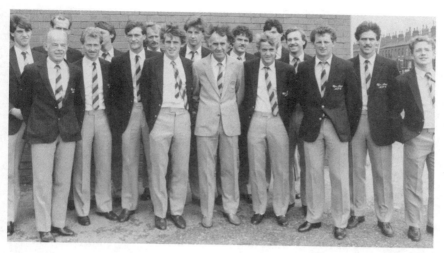

Harry McNally and Squad, 1983

with raising enough money through his Latics Lifeline campaign to see the club through to the start of the next season but McNally would be faced with the proposition of rebuilding the team on a shoestring. The new blood might be just what was needed to see better days return to Springfield Park.

1983/84

The 1983/84 season was a transitional spell for Wigan Athletic. Brian Heathcote had taken over the club from Pye and McNally was forced to bring in a host of young players on free transfers, including; 18-year-old striker Mike Newell who joined from Crewe; 19-year-old former Liverpool trainee Tony Kelly who earned the nickname 'Zico' for his prowess in dead ball situations; and 17-year-old Paul Cook who signed from non-league Marine. 18-year-old David Lowe, a former apprentice who signed professional forms for the club in the pre-season, was another player to add to this list. Not only would the four be great servants to the club. They would also play a major part in keeping it afloat when each was sold on at huge profit in years to come. The club was in no way out of the financial mire and would not be until Dave Whelan appeared on the scene some eleven years later.

Journalist Harold Ashurst concurs:

"As soon as Ken Cowap had sold his shares to Pye in the early 1980s a

Left to right: Alex Cribley, Paul Butler, Tony Kelly, Graham Barrow, Neil Bailey.

period of great instability set in that only ended when Whelan took over the club."

Persistent problems off the field, however, did not taint some progress on it. McNally raised the spirit in the dressing room and got the players playing for each other again. The youth he'd brought into the club played an integral part in that and though he would not be around to witness it, he had the makings of a team that would go all the way to Wembley the following season to lift the club's first silverware in the League era.

That was in the future. Wigan Athletic had to maintain its Third Division status first. McNally's team took seven attempts to register its first win in the 1983/84 season, during which time it was eliminated from the League Cup in the first round by Bury. The club's first precious league win did not mark a change in form. It only won four of its next 15 games, including a 4-2 home win against Bradford in the FA Cup first round. By this time it was a lowly fifteenth in the league.

It was far from being the perfect start and by Christmas the club was placed in seventeenth position. It was, though, still in the FA Cup courtesy of a 1-0 home win against non-league Whitby Town. The reward for that victory was a tasty third round tie against West Ham at Upton Park. The Latics would go down 1-0 in the tie despite a battling performance that would later begin to characterise the side.

It wasn't to be their year in the league. The team won just ten of its 25 games in the New Year. The indifferent form was typical of the season and the club finished fifteenth. Still, the young Latics side were establishing themselves in the division and a determination returned to the side that, given time, would be matched with consistency. Observers at the time noted that with the addition of a little experience the team could go far.

1984/85

With some promising youngsters already attracting the attention of top flight clubs, the 1984/85 season was much anticipated by club and fans alike. In Newell, Kelly and Lowe they had some class performers waiting to come of age. The Latics were able to add to the squad in the close season too and even paid £15,000 to bring in 20-year-old Paul Jewell from Liverpool before Christmas. Jewell's signing is thought to have been made possible by an FA Cup run that saw the Latics beat Wrexham and Norwich Victoria to set up a money-spinning third round tie against Chelsea, and a League Cup campaign including ties with Wrexham and West Brom.

League form that season was as indifferent as the year before, however. By Christmas the Latics found themselves in familiar territory and despite a looming FA Cup third round tie with old adversaries Chelsea, pressure was mounting on McNally. On January 5, 1985 the club recorded a memorable 2-2 draw with the west London club. The replay at Springfield Park brought in much needed revenue. However, the club went down 5-0 to the visitors on January 26.

McNally clung onto his job for another few weeks but after going seven games without a win, and with the club sitting a disappointing fifteenth in the table, McNally's time at the club was up. Bryan Hamilton, who had just been sacked by Tranmere Rovers was contacted about the vacancy and hired almost immediately. It would be the first of two spells at the club for the convivial Ulsterman.

"I'd only just been sacked at Tranmere in February when I was asked across to meet Heathcote," says Hamilton who now works as a broadcaster for *Eurosport*, *Setanta*, and *BBC Five Live*. "He told me that the club had no money but that it would be a challenge so I took the job. Getting sacked at Tranmere had been a blow because I'd invested so much time and effort in the club. I'd been asked to buy and sell players just to keep the club going. When I went to Wigan I told them that I was a coach and that I'd like to do just that. I never ended up buying or selling anybody during my first spell there.

"I was looking forward to working at Wigan because they were getting gates of between 3-4,000. That was quite a bit down from what they'd first got into the league right enough, but at Tranmere we were only getting 1,500. There was definite potential there."

The league was a lost cause by the time Hamilton joined with the Latics limping home in sixteenth position. But those first few months were a happy time for both him and the club's supporters with the Freight Rover Trophy, a cup competition contested by Division Three and Four teams, allowing the young team to finally make its mark on the 1984/85 season. By the time Hamilton had joined on March 1, 1985 the club had already overcome Wrexham in the first round of the competition.

With a few tweaks to the squad, Hamilton took the team on an unprecedented cup run.

"Harry had assembled a good group of players and all I did was change the shape of them a little bit. They were terrific lads who were prepared to try something new. David Lowe was playing outside right and I moved him across to the left wing to give the team a better balance. Everyone joined in and did marvellously.

"I later took Ian Griffiths on a free transfer and he played on the left so I could move Lowe back over to the right. Barrow played up front and the likes of Newell, Kelly, Langley, Jewell, Methven, Warren Aspinall and John Butler, gave us a great blend of youth and experience."

Wigan Athletic went on to beat Bury 1-0 in the second round of the competition just one month after Hamilton took over. A quarter final (North) against Tranmere Rovers nine days later went Wigan's way again. After beating Hamilton's former club 3-1, with goals from the team's young strike force of Lowe (2) and Kelly, the fans started dreaming of Wembley. After the miserable time the club and fans had been through since reaching Division Three they were allowed to dream just a little.

The Latics played Lincoln City in the semi final (North) of the Freight Rover Trophy and again won by a 3-1 margin. The Latics were one step closer to a fairytale Wembley final. Hamilton had brought cup fever back to Wigan in just a few short months there. He remembers the time with some affection.

"We went on a fantastic run and it was arguably the happiest time of my management career."

Ian Halliwell has fond memories of the respite that the cup run brought.

"Under Hamilton we had the best team we'd almost ever had. Newell, Lowe and Steve Walsh were all class players and the cup run injected some excitement into following the club again."

The Latics met Mansfield Town on May 20 in the Northern Final of the Freight Rover Trophy with a place in the final-proper in Wembley at stake. It was the toughest tie of the competition for the club and only a fortuitous own goal earned the team a draw over the 90 minutes before they went on to beat their tricky opponents 3-1 on penalties. Few people at the club or on the terraces could believe that after two depressing seasons they had a day out at Wembley to look forward to.

Wigan Athletic went into the final against Brentford on June 1 as rank outsiders. It was a great day for the many thousands of fans who made the journey down for the club's first appointment at the national stadium since their disappointing loss to Scarborough in the 1973 FA Trophy.

The Freight Rover was a cut above. This was a Football League competition. The players were as excited as the fans to have the chance of bringing home a precious piece of League silverware

Paul Jewell (front left) with the squad that won the 1985 Freight Rover Trophy.

The final scoreboard, 1985 Freight Rover Trophy.

"It was great for the fans to go to Wembley but it was great for us too. We both deserved our day out there," recalls David Lowe.

Goals by Newell, Kelly and a Lowe wonder strike sealed a 3-1 win over a Brentford side that had finished three places above the Latics in the league that season. Lowe would be a hero on the day but in his own words his performance left a lot to be desired.

"I scored an overhead kick in the final but it was the first kick I'd had all match. It was probably the last too. I didn't have a very good game but no-one remembers that."

No-one would remember either the poor league form of that season or the club's problems off the pitch. Wigan Athletic had lifted a trophy at Wembley after just seven seasons in the League and they deserved to savour it. If Hamilton could keep the promising young team together the sky was the limit.

7   REASONS FOR OPTIMISM

It's amazing what a bit of silverware in the trophy cabinet will do for morale. Everything seemed sunny at Springfield Park. There was every reason for optimism. Hamilton's team was laced with talented young players who were destined to play at a higher level. Whether this was with the Latics as they climbed the League ladder or elsewhere was undecided. Off the field, Bill Kenyon had bought his way into the boardroom and it seemed to the fans that they could look forward to a successful season. Players such as Alex Cribley were not so sure that Kenyon's arrival would promise the financial shot in the arm the club needed.

"When Kenyon took over he came in for the first meeting with the team and said, 'I'll guarantee the wages for the first month'. We were thinking, 'Ok. But what about after that?' As the season got underway we never not got paid but we did get paid late quite a lot. When we saw the club going that way so quickly after Kenyon became involved you did ask yourself what was in store in the future."

Harold Ashurst recalls that Kenyon's tenure at the club was doomed to failure from the very beginning.

"Kenyon had fantastic ambitions for Wigan Athletic but the bottom line was that he didn't have the necessary funding to take the club forward."

Hamilton's Wembley victors kicked off the season with three wins on the trot. The highlight was the League Cup first round, first leg win over Port Vale on August 20, 1985. The club's good start continued and by September it was a permanent fixture in the top three. Early October saw the good form persist but the club started to slide down the table towards the end of the month. They would also go out of the League Cup as Port Vale turned over the one goal deficit in the second leg. As the club experienced the first blip of the season, crowds at Springfield Park started to recede again. It didn't help the financial problems that had stalked the club since they'd overspent so wildly to get into Division Three.

"The club's finances weren't solved suddenly by us winning the Freight Rover Trophy," recalls Bryan Hamilton. "The club was living hand to mouth all the time and the gates weren't improving. At the start of my second season we were third in the table. We were playing the team who were second top.

I was really looking forward to it and thought we'd get a massive crowd but we got 3,000. I couldn't understand it. We needed bigger crowds more than ever then. We were getting between 2,000 to 3,000 by November. I remember thinking then that it was going to take an awful lot to change it.

"But you couldn't blame the fans. At that time Springfield Park was very sad. It wasn't a nice place to watch football. It was tired and maintaining and updating it was becoming very expensive which contributed to the state we were in. The training facilities were non-existent too. We trained at Robin Park and relied on the local council to cut the grass. They were feeling the pinch then too so sometimes instead of cutting the whole pitch they'd cut an outline along the sideline, the halfway line and the 18 yard box and that was it. It was a tough time for the club."

We trained at Robin Park and relied on the local council to cut the grass

November and December saw more of the same for the Latics both on and off the park. The club were sitting eighth in the table after a patchy few games in early December. After losing 1-0 to Derby in the league on December 22, the Latics staged a comeback and went on a 14 match unbeaten league run. They were not beaten until March 29, 1986 and the run saw the club hit second spot. From such a good position and with such a decent team, the club really should have won promotion that season. It was a travesty that it didn't. The Latics finished fourth, just one point shy of third place and a precious promotion to Division Two.

The club could take some comfort from a decent FA Cup run, however. It would equal the club record of reaching the fourth round, though the Latics could do nothing to avoid being beaten by Southampton at The Dell by three goals to nil.

The Freight Rover Trophy again proved a hit with the Latics but it was a case of close but no cigar. After the success of the year before the club almost reached the Wembley final for a second time. It was not to be and Bolton Wanderers knocked Wigan Athletic out in the Northern Final.

The shine was well and truly taken off the team's coming of age when news broke that star striker Mike Newell was to be sold. He wouldn't be the last. In fact many argued that the club could have gone further in the league

Bryan Hamilton receives the Manager of the Month Award

and both cups that season had the squad been kept intact. After Newell, who had scored 16 goals in 24 games for the club that season, was sold to Luton for £100,000, Warren Aspinall (£150,000 to Everton, Feb 4, 1986) and Tony Kelly (£80,000 to Stoke, April 26, 1986) soon followed him out the exit door.

To be fair to the club they had been under pressure from when the very first ball of the campaign was kicked. That it took until January 9, 1986 until its first player was sold was a credit to it. The fans and Newell's fellow players saw things differently, however.

"Newell going was a huge disappointment to the senior players in that team," recalls Graham Barrow. "We finished fourth in the league that season and there weren't any play-offs but if we'd kept Newell, Aspinall and Kelly we would almost certainly have got promotion. The worse thing was that a lot of the players were sold off quite cheaply. If £100,000 was mentioned they'd be off. If we'd held onto the likes of Newell and Walsh for another season the club would have benefited on the field and you would have been talking £500,000 each. It would have solved a lot of the problems off the field. The most frustrating thing is that Wigan could have tasted success the hard way long before Dave Whelan came onto the scene. That team from 1984/85 could have achieved more if it had stayed intact."

Alex Cribley was a little more understanding of the situation.

"We had to sell because the club was skint. It was disheartening but we just got on with it. There was no choice. At least we'd know once someone went that we'd be getting paid and the club would have a reprieve for a while."

Harold Ashurst recalls the frustration that the fire sale caused.

"The fans were irate. If the Latics could have kept that team together they could have got promoted with ease the following season. It was disappointing when you saw the proceeds going to pay off debts. The lack of ambition was there for all to see."

Hamilton is much derided for breaking up the side, and for selling off even more players when he returned for a second spell at the club three years later. As he explains, it saddened no-one more than him to have to dismantle the promising squad.

"I'm sorry we didn't get promotion. It could have happened but for the circumstances. Of course it was frustrating to see all the best players going. I didn't want to sell Newell. That was a major mistake and I got none of the £100,000 to strengthen the team. I respected the directors at the time though. They loved the club but they didn't have the money you'd normally associate with a director.

"Because of this, money was always going to be a factor when big clubs did eventually start knocking on the door. I admit that I found it difficult when someone would come in for a player. I thought they deserved to know. How could I deny them a move to a bigger club when they'd given such good service to the club?

"All this was irrelevant anyway. There was nothing we could do when a club came in for a player because we didn't have the resources to keep them. We tried to do the best we could under the circumstances. We kept taking young

The writing seemed to be on the wall for a decaying Springfield Park

players into the side to replace them and got on with it."

It seems that Hamilton really did have his hands tied. The fans had a right to be angry, especially those that faithfully watched the club through thick and thin. To them it seemed like the club was going down a one way street from which it would never return.

The writing seemed to be on the wall for a decaying Springfield Park too. This was another bone of contention for the fans who saw a move away from Springy as tantamount to disaster. It didn't help when the Taylor Report cut

Brenda Spencer (Wigan Athletic's current Chief Executive)

the capacity at the ground from 20,000 to 10,800. Still, based on the average gate of the day, getting a full house would in itself be an achievement.

The Kenyon era would ultimately start a process which would ring the death knell for a badly decaying Springfield Park. By February 1986 Kenyon had already voiced his intention to replace it with a 15,000 seater stadium replete with leisure complex, restaurant and shops (sound familiar?). There was also the seed of a controversial plan to move the club to a new stadium in Skelmersdale. To the relief of the fans, this idea never got off the drawing board.

Brenda Spencer, who was hired as club accountant by Kenyon and remains at the club today, remembers that Kenyon's ideas were bigger than his wallet.

"Bill didn't have the financial clout to properly back the club. He was looking at ways and means of making things better, including moving grounds which was his dream, but he didn't have the finance to see those plans through to fruition."

Kenyon's plans would never be more than pipe dreams. But, with Springfield Park by now having been earmarked as prime Lancashire real estate as a property boom swept the country, the club would before long secure its overdraft against the value of the stadium. It seemed a case of if and not when the club would be forced to sell its only real off field asset. The fans would have to get used to the idea. In time they'd learn that their beloved stadium was one of the main things that had been holding the club back.

Hamilton left Wigan Athletic at the end of the 1985/86 season for Leicester City. The top flight club were impressed with what Hamilton had achieved on a shoestring even if Latics fans were not. Hamilton's first act as Foxes manager did not do much to endear him further. He was to cherry pick one of the Latics' rising young stars. Hamilton's actions weren't completely selfish, however.

"When I moved to Leicester I bought Steve Walsh from Wigan for £100,000. I knew that the club was struggling for money and that he was a good player. I pondered it for a while but thought:

A. it will ease Wigan's financial problems;

B. it will help Leicester;

and C. it will help Steve Walsh."

The fans didn't like it but they were going to have to get used to seeing their best players leave. It wasn't all doom and gloom. The Latics had lost a handful of their top young players but the backbone of the squad still remained. Players like Paul Cook, Paul Jewell and David Lowe were raring to go for the new season while seasoned campaigners like Bobby Campbell and David Hamilton joined to add some more experience.

David Hamilton was left in no doubt as to where football came in the minds of Wiganers when he'd come to look around the club before signing.

"When I first came to Wigan I had to ask directions to the football club. Twice I was sent to Central Park. I said, 'No, I mean the football club'. That is what 'football' was to people there. Rugby League Football. The rugby team had 13 internationals playing for them and were getting 20,000 per week at Central Park. That says everything about what the Latics have always been up against."

1986/87

The sale of Steve Walsh to Leicester told the fans and players all they needed to know about their club's resources. It seemed to be a never ending soap opera. The 1986/87 season was barely a week old when the first dreaded collection buckets appeared on the terraces to raise money for the players' wages. They would become a permanent fixture on the terraces for the foreseeable future. To their credit, the fans always put their hands in their pockets and their contributions were relied upon by the club more than they could have imagined.

Brenda Spencer was all too aware of the predicament the club was in:

"We were desperate for money. It was as simple as that. The money went toward keeping the club ticking over."

Ray Mathias took over from Hamilton in June 1986. The squad really wasn't in terrible shape, though it desperately needed a season-long respite from selling players. It wasn't to be.

"My first job as manager was to sell Kevin Langley to Everton. That told me how it was going to be that season," says Mathias.

Mathias' team didn't get off to the start he'd have hoped for. They'd been buoyed by coming so close to being promoted the season before and felt that it was well within their grasp during the coming campaign. Mathias inspired confidence in the squad too. He would become a fans' favourite in time.

The Latics lost their first six games in the 1986/87 season. Their League Cup hoodoo continued too. They were knocked out by Blackburn Rovers in the first round. The Freight Rover Trophy, a competition that the Latics felt a

Springfield Park

degree of ownership over after winning and being losing semi-finalists in the last two seasons, was not as good to the club as it had been in the past. Bury dumped Wigan out unceremoniously in the early rounds.

Before its FA Cup first round tie against Lincoln City, the Latics won seven of its twelve league matches. By November 8 they sat tenth in Division Three but, crucially, hadn't yet sold any more players. With a play-off structure being introduced for the first time that season there was everything to play for and the board of directors and staff worked overtime to keep the club ticking over, organising fund-raising events, collections, and juggling overdue bills.

Wigan Athletic made short shrift of Lincoln City in the FA Cup and hammered Darlington 5-0 in the second round. The Fans crossed their fingers that another lengthy cup run was in the makings. These back to back victories formed the foundations for a 16 match unbeaten run in all competitions. During this time the Latics beat Gillingham, Norwich City and Hull City in the FA Cup to set up an historic quarter final against Leeds Utd at Springfield Park.

Manager Ray Mathias was stunned by the hysteria that swept through the town ahead of the match.

"When we played Leeds there were 13,000 plus there. It was bursting at the seams. On the day the town had to be closed off. So many people wanted to go to the game but the stadium just couldn't accommodate them."

Leeds would beat the Latics 2-0 at Springfield Park. Mathias still thinks the Latics should have won.

"It was very harsh. It should have gone in our favour with the chances we had."

The defeat left the fans wondering what could have been if they'd not sold Aspinall, Kelly, Newell and Walsh who were all successfully plying their trades in higher leagues. The feeling deepened when the Latics went on another decent run in the league. They lost only two out of their final 17 games that season to finish fourth and set up an historic play off with third place Swindon Town.

The winner of the Wigan versus Swindon tie would face relegated Sunderland for a place in the Second Division. A slightly disappointing 6,718 turned out at Springfield Park to watch the Latics go down 3-2 to Swindon in what was arguably as important a match as the Leeds Utd cup semi final. The Latics were two nil up after 15 minutes but conceded three in a desperate last 18 minutes to lose by the odd goal. The team was devastated.

A packed house for the FA Cup 6th Round against Leeds United, Springfield Park

"In the return leg at Swindon we went for it and slaughtered them," recalls Mathias. "We hit the post, hit the bar, but couldn't get the ball in the net and went out 3-2 on aggregate. It was a big blow to the team. Some of the players found it hard to accept that we'd been beaten. Chris Thompson couldn't understand it. He went missing for two days. He was so disappointed. His wife called me but I didn't know where he was. No-one knows to this day. It was a difficult time because the players had put everything into getting to the play-offs and we'd seen a lot of good players leave that season too."

Another chance of promotion had slipped through the club's fingers. David Hamilton, who scored in the first leg against Swindon, remembers how it could have all been so different.

"If we could have brought in even a couple more players that season we could have done better in the play-offs. If Wigan had had money behind them then when they'd built two really good teams they could have pushed on. That was how close we were to success but the chairman's pockets weren't deep enough and there just wasn't the revenue from the turnstiles to finance it. For example, we played Leeds in the FA Cup on a Sunday and there were 13,000 at Springfield Park. We were top of the league and we played Chesterfield midweek and there were 2,500 there. You can imagine how the chairman and the players felt."

Relations between the terraces and boardroom were not brightened when David Lowe followed Newell and Co. out the door at the end of the season. Lowe claims to have left for footballing reasons but with two months of the close season with no income looming it is more likely that the £80,000 offered by Ipswich was too good to refuse.

Light relief came during the 1986/87 season from a story which was broken in the local papers about Mikhail Gorbachev being a Latics fan. For a club bereft of celebrity fans it was a fact to revel in. It was an unlikely story and there were many explanations as to how the Soviet president had come to support a town from deepest, darkest Lancashire. John Fillingham, the club's commercial manager, tried to take responsibility for the urban myth, telling the *Sunday Times* no less, "The chairman and I came up with a tale about Gorbachev being a Wigan supporter. Wigan once played Moscow Dynamo and our line was that ever since then Gorbachev had been a devout fan."

But the real man behind the story was local reporter Harold Ashurst. The story sounded unlikely because it was. It was a hoax, but one that Ashurst was only too happy to exploit.

"I admit it. I broke the Gorbachev story. One of director Stan Jackson's friends had been seen an article in the *South China Morning Post* about

Paul Jewell scores the winner against Norwich, FA Cup 4th Round, January 1st 1987

Gorbachev. At the end of the article it said, 'Not many people know that Gorbachev is a Wigan Athletic supporter'. The couple, who ran an off-licence in Newton-le-Willows, gave the paper to Stan who gave it to me.

"I rang the Russian embassy who knew nothing about it. I rang the journalist who'd written the article. He said that when he got to the end of the article he wanted to say who the president supported but didn't have a clue so he opened up an English newspaper and saw the name Wigan Athletic and put it down. Not to let the facts spoil a good story we ran with it and got a quote from the Russian embassy saying, 'Mr Gorbachev wishes Wigan all the success in the cup tie with Leeds'."

Mr Gorbachev wishes Wigan all the success in the cup tie with Leeds

Later, another rumour would come to light about Gorbachev being secretary of a Russian team the club played in the 1970s but there was no truth in that at all. Another rumour stated that Gorbachev had visited the Heinz factory in the town and been presented with a Latics shirt. Again this story was proven to be a fake. A further rumour said that Gorbachev would suspend the Soviet ban on foreign radio for 90 minutes every time a Latics match was on BBC. Again there was no truth in the matter. The myth persists to this day.

If it makes depressing reading to hear about the never ending financial struggles of Wigan Athletic imagine what it was like to live through it? Nothing changed for Wigan off the field between 1981 and 1994 when Dave Whelan took over. Different chairmen and owners came through the door with plans to change the fortunes of the club but no-one ever did. It was a case of different name, different season, same old story.

Brenda Spencer is credited with working tirelessly to keep the club afloat in the 1980s and early 1990s when she was club accountant, football secretary and did any number of other tasks. Her reward was to be appointed chief executive when Dave Whelan took over the club in 1995. Today she writes cheques for £5m for players without batting an eyelid.

Spencer is one of the few people qualified to say what really went on behind closed doors during the club's darkest hours. As Ashurst says jokingly:

"Brenda knows where the bodies are buried!"

Curiously, despite seeing the club nearly go out of business on more than one occasion, Spencer wouldn't have had it any other way.

"Bill Kenyon brought me in as accountant at the club. I was looking after all the financial affairs and became football secretary too. At one time I tried to do everything and I worked all hours. In the 1980s the financial state of the club was bad. There were times when the club would have folded if it weren't for the willingness of the directors, the fans and other benefactors to dig into their own pockets. I'd never be without those days though because the struggle seemed to form a special bond between the club and those who did everything they could to keep it afloat."

Not all fans agree with Spencer. It was impossible to see the big picture back then. The club was struggling but it had been struggling for years and would go on to struggle ad infinitum was the view of most. Most of the fair-weather fans had deserted the terraces by the late 1980s anyway. Ironically that was precisely the type of fan that the club needed to win back,. The hardcore of 1,500 that remained in the stands at Springfield Park would be there week in week out whether the club was playing Manchester United or Northwich Victoria reserves. It was no less painful for them, however, to see the club's dip in form after twice coming so close to promotion.

1987/88

The 1987/88 season was a particularly poor time for cup competition at Springfield Park. The Latics acquiesced to Wolves in the second round of the FA Cup, went out of the League Cup in the same round, and crashed out of the Freight Rover Trophy in the second preliminary round.

League form wasn't terrible that season. In fact the club got off to a great start. The Latics were unbeaten in their first seven matches and were top of the table at the end of September. It then took the club eight attempts to record their next victory during which time they slipped to eleventh in the Barclays Third Division. Between December 12 and February 6 the club went ten games undefeated to climb back up to third spot. The club wouldn't repeat that form again during the 1987/88 campaign, however, and despite bringing in Dave Thompson, Allen Tankard and Neill Rimmer, after seeing Paul Cook join Norwich, the club lost its last four league games to finish seventh.

It really wasn't a bad result on the face of it and should have gone a long

A penalty miss in the final game of the 1987/8 season. Wigan Athletic 0 Grimsby Town 1

way to consolidating the club in the league. Yet the fans knew that a virtually identical team had come within a whisker of promotion the year before and they were entitled to be disgruntled. The fans may have been glad to see another disappointing campaign end but one person who was not was Spencer.

"At the end of every season I used to be so nervous about whether we'd survive until the start of the next. We didn't have any money coming in during the summer because there weren't any games. The directors mostly kept the club going through times like these. We had to rely on the people who we owed money bearing with us too. Our coach company, for example, would let us chip away at our bill throughout the season At the time I said I was going to write a book of excuses for not paying bills. The relationship we had with our suppliers was important though. People appreciated that we were trying our best and somehow we always got ourselves out of it in the end. The wage bill may only have been £5,000 but we just didn't have it."

Current club physio Alex Cribley, who suffered a career-ending injury during the 1987/88 season, confirms that the club was down to the bare bones.

"After retiring from the game, Ray Mathias hired me as club physio. He said I'd have to muck in and do a bit of everything. There was only Ray, Dave Philpotts who took the kids and me – who did the kids, the match kit, the boots and looked after the injuries on staff. Dave Crompton was on the payroll part-time too. That was it. That was the coaching and backroom staff."

The skeleton staff that Cribley joined would barely have been big enough to run a Saturday morning youth side let alone a full-time League club. It was going to require a sea change at the club to turn things around and, in the following six seasons things would go from bad to worse both on and off the field to leave the club at the lowest ebb in its history.

7 SELLING THE CROWN JEWELS

If seventh place in the Barclays Third Division was not good enough for the Latics faithful the season before, a bottom half finish in the 1988/89 season was certainly never going to be. By March 11, 1989 the Latics were languishing third from bottom of the table, and were out or on their way out of the FA Cup, League Cup and Sherpa Van Trophy (formerly the Freight Rover Trophy). The club had already off-loaded Paul Jewell (£80,000 to Bradford), John Butler (£75,000 to Stoke) and Andy Holden (£130,000 to Oldham) in order to pay off spiralling debts. Mathias had done his best for the club but was as frustrated as anyone at seeing his star players leave for a song.

"I had to sell Jewell to Bradford City for £80,000. I knew he was worth more than that but because of the situation we were in it was hard to negotiate. People knew we were desperate for the money."

The sales left the Latics with a squad of inexperienced players. Mathias, who was running out of time at the club recalls the surprise one victory that season caused.

"My last season there it was just a matter of survival. I remember going to Mansfield in January. We had a load of kids in the squad. Peter Atherton and Joe Parkinson were making their debuts. Our one experienced pro at the time was Mark Hilditch. I gave my team talk, saying how we were going to hammer Mansfield, and I saw Mark looking round the room at all the young players. He was stunned at the lack of experience. We eventually won the match with Joe Parkinson scoring the winner. Mark was jumping up and down in the dressing room after."

But Mathias would not see out the season. Here for the first time Mathias reveals why he parted ways with the club he'd grown to love.

"We had good youngsters but they were never going to win promotion. We had no money to bring anyone in and there was lots of disruption behind the scenes. Kenyon came to me and said he wanted to bring someone in to help me out. I told him we were okay. It had been a selling season but I told him it would get better. We were seventh from bottom in the league but I knew we wouldn't go down. But he insisted and he left me no choice. He said, 'Either I bring someone in to work with you or you can leave'. So I left."

Ray Woods joined as a player just before Mathias left and wasn't encouraged by what he saw.

"Mathias asked me if I wanted to sign for Wigan," says Woods in an interview on the official PFA website. "However, they couldn't afford to pay Colne the £500 fee they wanted so they asked me if I'd pay it and then Wigan would reimburse me in installments! I said 'No chance'."

> They couldn't afford to pay Colne the £500 fee... they asked me if I'd pay it

Woods eventually joined the young squad on a free transfer after Colne failed to register the player properly with the FA. He'd miss the entire season after picking up an injury but did return for the club's fabled, inaugural pre-season trip to Russia.

"We only drank Coke all week and when we asked for potatoes with our meals it was as though we had asked for the crown jewels! We all returned undernourished and knackered."

It's not clear whether Mikhail Gorbachev came to watch the Latics on their tour. Maybe he listened to the matches on the radio. He was probably otherwise occupied, working to end the cold war.

One player going the opposite way out of the club as Woods joined was David Hamilton.

"When it came to signing a new deal I said, 'No, you're selling all the best players'. I didn't like what they'd done to Mathias either. He'd done a great job. The situation at the club turned everyone but the diehard off."

That was an understatement.

With the fans still smarting from the loss of the popular Mathias, into the fray stepped Bryan Hamilton who'd just been sacked by Leicester City. As the man the fans held responsible for the break up of one of the club's greatest ever teams, he wasn't exactly welcomed back with open arms.

Hamilton would steady the Latics ship that season, however, helping the club bounce back from the fringes of the relegation zone to finish the season in seventeenth place. It would be his exploits from then on that would make him a hate figure in the town. By the end of his four year reign the Latics would be hurtling uncontrollably towards relegation and financial ruin.

David Hamilton and Bill Kenyon

1989/90

Bryan Hamilton knew he was accepting a poisoned chalice when he took the Wigan Athletic job. In the coming seasons he would be forced to sell numerous key players, bringing in over £1m to keep the club afloat. The fans only saw the negative side, however. They never stopped to consider that Hamilton was a reluctant participant in this process. All they knew were the rumours they'd heard that Hamilton was receiving a percentage of the sales. Many thought he was selling players purely to line his own pockets. Nothing could have been further from the truth.

"I'd just lost my job with Leicester and I wasn't really looking to get another job in football immediately," says Hamilton. "Wigan had been good to me when I'd been there before and they were very helpful when I'd had a chance to go to Leicester so I was happy to consider going back. They were in trouble, though. They were desperately short of money and were having trouble selling players. It was going to be a case of keeping the club alive. They wanted me to oversee the development of young players so we put Dave Crompton full-time to run that. We tried to copy the Crewe model. That was to develop players, make sure there was always a decent team on the pitch and, if need be, to sell players to fund the whole operation.

"When I joined from Leicester I'd been on First Division money. What Wigan offered me just wasn't enough. So they put together a package with a bonus structure linked to how well I did in developing and selling on players. It wasn't what I wanted and I told them I'd prefer the straight salary but they couldn't afford that so I had a decision to make.

"It wasn't an uncommon practice but it was relatively new. Dario Gradi had done it for years at Crewe and Iain Dowie recently said it had been part of his contract at Crystal Palace. What happened was that I did better with the transfer fees than they'd anticipated. I knew so many people in the game and they respected my opinion on the quality players. I could negotiate a decent package for the football club. Because I did better than expected it created a complication for everyone involved.

"It became an embarrassment to us all after that. I tried to get them to change to offer me the salary I wanted and remove the incentives. Eventually they got to that stage but it took a while. It was a very difficult situation for me personally. You have to remember that I'd been sacked at Tranmere for refusing to do the same thing.

"It was a very difficult situation. I was trying to keep the semblance of a side together but at the same time trying to fund the whole operation. I concentrated on developing players and if clubs came in and asked about them we'd move them on for the most we could get. I trusted the board to return funds to me to improve things on the field if there was anything left over from paying off debts. I couldn't say I enjoyed that time. It wasn't what I wanted to do. I won't criticise anyone for doing it though. The directors were doing the best they could."

Anyone who has met Hamilton will be left in no doubt as to the veracity of his account. The fans were entitled to adopt him as scapegoat for what was happening at the club but they had to face up to the reality that the Latics were entering a period of financial meltdown that would make the club's previous problems pale into insignificance.

"The bank started to put the club under pressure around the time Hamilton came back," says club auditor Ian Halliwell. "The only assets the club had were the ground and the players. The bank had lent against the value of the ground on the back of the early 1980s property boom but when that collapsed in the late 1980s the negative equity put a massive strain on the club's finances. It was the final straw and they lost fiscal control."

Harold Ashurst covered the Hamilton saga for the local press. He'd never seen things so bad at the club.

"It was a low point in my time following the club but it's wrong to say that the characters involved were unsavoury because that would imply that they were crooks and criminals. They weren't."

Some, like former Wigan Athletic player and current Chester assistant manager Graham Barrow, are less forgiving of Hamilton.

"Taking a percentage for a player is something I have never or would never do because as a manager you should always be focused on building a team, not breaking it up."

That also summed up the attitude of the fans but Hamilton stuck resolutely to his unpleasant but necessary task. Actually, only two notable players were sold during the 1989/90 season – Paul Beesley for £175,000 to Leyton Orient and Neil Whitworth for £150,000 to Manchester Utd – but in a team that found itself battling relegation they could have made all the difference. The club would only just avoid the drop after taking just three points from its last nine games. It felt like winning the league after a season that had seen the club rock bottom just a few months earlier.

The Latics did better in cup competition. They got to the third round of the FA Cup only to be beaten by Watford. The Latics also reached the quarter final of the Leyland DAF Cup (formerly the Freight Rover Trophy) only to lose after extra time to Doncaster Rovers. In the League Cup, they got a plum tie in the second round when they drew Liverpool, who were dominating English football at the time. The draw brought an unwelcome reminder of the club's predicament, however.

"The stadium was eating up a lot of money at the time but the final straw was when we couldn't play Liverpool there because the ground was unsafe," recalls Hamilton. "Around that time we were doing tours of Springfield Park to raise some money but it got to the stage where I stopped people coming into the dressing room because it was run down, sad and not as hygienic as it should be. The whole club needed help."

1990/91

Before a ball had even been kicked in the 1990/91 season Wigan Athletic had sold David Thompson to Preston for £77,500. The proceeds would buy the club some breathing space and Hamilton wouldn't be required to sell a player again until early in the New Year.

The players welcomed the temporary respite but the club still got off to a typically mixed start that season. By December 1 the Latics were trailing in the bottom half of the Barclays Third Division. The club were out of the League Cup by this time but were at the beginning of a decent FA Cup campaign. The Latics always seemed to be able to raise their game in the competition.

An FA Cup first round 5-1 drubbing of Carlisle United set up a home tie with Hartlepool United. Wigan came out on top in that December 8 clash, by which time they'd still not been able to climb from fifteenth in the league. All attention was now on the draw for the FA Cup third round. First Division Coventry City were pulled out of the hat in a tie that would see the Latics play at the top flight club's ground on January 5. On that bitterly cold winter's day the Latics soon found themselves 1-0 down. As the match went on it seemed less and less likely that the club could get themselves back into the game. Then, with barely a few seconds on the clock, Ray Woods swung in an inch perfect cross for Darren Patterson to head past the imposing Steve Ogrizovic. It was a great moment for the fans who deserved a bit of good news. The game clearly didn't do Woods any harm. He'd be sold to Coventry before the month was out for £200,000.

Wigan's last gasp equaliser earned the club a replay back at Springfield Park. BBC showed the game live and the revenue enabled the club not to have to sell any more first team members for the remainder of the season. Despite putting up a spirited performance, the Latics could not overcome the First Division club and lost 1-0 in a game that could have gone either way.

The club also had a good Leyland DAF Cup run and conceded only twice in the first four rounds before being dumped out by three goals to nil by Tranmere Rovers in the Northern semi final. In the league, the Latics started the New Year in a familiar seventeenth position and it looked like they were heading for a lower bottom half finish, if not relegation. But after the New Year's Day loss to Huddersfield, the club lost just one of its next ten fixtures to climb to twelfth in the league by March 9, 1991. Wigan Athletic won seven, drew three and lost five of its remaining 15 matches and ended the year a respectable tenth. It was better than could have been hoped for after a poor start to the season and was the club's highest finish in the league for three years. To the fans it still reeked of mediocrity.

By his third year back in charge, Hamilton was resigning himself to the reality that faced the club.

"Football was never top of the agenda at board meetings. It was always the finances. Peter Atherton was a fantastic player but Coventry liked him so it looked ominous as the board met in the close season. All I could do once everybody agreed that it was going to happen was try and get the most money possible for the player. We got £300,000 and it was all swallowed up by the club. We had to replace him for nothing and hope that we could sell the replacement too. It seemed that the funds from the players I'd previously sold had changed nothing. It just meant the club was still in business. We were no further forward as the 1991/92 season started as when I'd joined in 1989."

1991/92

Kenyon was coming under increased pressure due to the state of the club as the 1991/92 season commenced. His fledgling plan to build a new stadium on the site of Springfield Park was no further forward. Nor was a more controversial plan to move the Latics out of Wigan. Kenyon must have wished as many people came to the games each week as objected to his plans for the new stadium.

Things looked promising for Wigan Athletic in the FA Cup that season. Again the competition provided a touch of glamour in a forgettable, trophy-less campaign. The Latics beat Scarborough 2-0 away in the first round. Stockport were dispatched by an identical scoreline in the next before Notts County beat the club 2-0 in the third round. It was that type of season. Wigan Athletic went out of the League Cup in the second round and the newly christened Autoglass Trophy (formerly the Freight Rover Trophy) was no more rewarding for the club. The Latics were knocked out in the preliminary rounds by Scarborough.

The 1991/92 league season was as mediocre as they come. The Latics failed to put together a winning run of more than three games all season but, similarly, never lost more than three in a row. Needless to say, the terraces were as empty as ever with crowds sometimes dipping below 1,000. But, despite being second from bottom by Boxing Day, the club bounced back to finish the year fifteenth in the Barclays Third Division. The club would play in the Barclays Second Division the following season as the old First Division was renamed the Barclays Premiership. Even the most hardcore fan could not view it as a promotion.

The season was given the fitting end it deserved when it was announced that Darren Paterson was leaving the club to join Crystal Palace for £225,000. With not one penny being made available to Hamilton to bolster his squad, even the most stubborn of fans must have realised by this stage that the club was in dire straits.

1992/93

It would be precisely one year before the Latics had to sell another prized asset. This had more to do with the fact that Kenyon would be succeeded by a new broom at Springfield Park than the finances, which remained on a knife edge. The season will be remembered for being Kenyon's last rather than for the club's performances on the field. In fact by the time that the new chairman and vice chairman, Stephen Gage and Nick Bitel, took over in March 1993 the club was residing third bottom of Barclays Division Two and was out of the FA and League Cups. The Latics did get to the Northern Final of the Autoglass Trophy but were denied a third date at Wembley after losing 3-2 to Stockport County.

Hamilton and his players took the loss to Stockport particularly hard.

Stephen Gage

Reaching the Northern Final of the competition had been scant consolation for a season that saw the club on a collision course with relegation. Some said it was overdue. In any case Bryan Hamilton had had enough.

"I couldn't say I enjoyed that time. It wasn't what I wanted to do. I wanted a football role. I discussed it with Kenyon during the season and he said he was trying to sell the club and said I if I was going to leave he would definitely do so."

Kenyon's time was up too and he did just that. Some fans were happy to see the back of him and his plans to relocate the club. It was inevitable. Brenda Spencer remembers that the new ownership didn't necessarily mean that the club's troubles were behind them, however:

Dave Philpotts

"Bill was bought out by a London consortium and they installed Stephen Gage and Nick Bitel to run the club. Stephen and Nick bought out the consortium soon after. The club started to become easier to run immediately because they were successful businessmen in their own right but the money was still a huge problem because we didn't get big crowds, didn't have many season ticket holders and couldn't charge much for sponsorship."

Gage and Bitel arrived at Springfield Park in early March 1993. The club was labouring at the foot of the league table but they asked Hamilton to stay on for an initial bedding-in period. Hamilton agreed, but would leave the club before it was finally relegated. He acknowledges that the damage was already done before Dave Philpotts took over as caretaker manager for the last few games of the season.

"I'd left just before we were relegated but I realised that I'd been part of it all. It was inevitable the way we were going. I'd told Gage long before that I wanted to leave and he'd accepted that."

Fans weren't sure what to expect from Gage, a southern businessman, and Bitel, a high-flying London lawyer. Some thought that, far from being the club's saviours, they were actually asset strippers. As top sports lawyer and chief executive of The London Marathon, Bitel explains, they were nothing of the sort.

"Kenyon sold the club to a financial investor that Stephen and I knew. I don't know if they knew what they were getting into or why they did it. It had seemed like a good idea at the time. They immediately offered us the chance to come in and take over the running of the club so we did and took over their shares a couple of months after. We took over the club's liabilities and paid a bit of money to the previous owner. We put some money into the club, which was needed. I'd been interested in football all my life and when the opportunity to get involved with a football club came up I got seduced into it."

Gage had similar motivations:

"Nick and I had a bit of a sporting background and thought it would a challenge and maybe even fun. I thought it would be a couple of days work a week but eventually I had to work full time at the club just to keep it going."

Gage had indeed taken on more than he'd anticipated. His memory of the club finances at the time sheds some light on the uphill struggle it would be to turn its fortunes around at that juncture.

"After Kenyon left there was a feeling in the town that things were really grim. People would stop me in the town and ask if the club would still be there in a week. I couldn't promise them anything because the club wasn't in brilliant condition. The DTI was doing an investigation into the shareholding in the club. The annual accounts were behind. We went in there with the aim of tidying everything up.

"We owed everyone money. We owed the Inland Revenue, VAT.... We owed a lot of people a little money so had to cut our cloths accordingly. The debts on a day-to-day basis weren't huge but there were lots of creditors. Hamilton had done a good job in helping the club service those debts. So much so that when we took over we were still getting payments for players he'd sold that had subsequently been sold on to Premiership clubs or played international games. The money that came in from transfers went straight toward the day-to-day running of the club and servicing the overdraft. We stopped the sale of players though."

We owed everyone money. We owed the Inland Revenue, VAT...

Bitel confirms that the transfer policy changed when they took the helm;

"In the time we were there we did not voluntarily sell a player. We sold Joe Parkinson to Bournemouth but we didn't want him to go and he only went after a tribunal. Bryan Hamilton got blamed when that type of thing happened. Allen Tankard also left for Port Vale and that went to tribunal too.

He was practically the last quality player we had at the club. They were not voluntary sales, however."

Two such high profile players leaving the club so soon after the new owners had taken over didn't instil confidence in the fans. Relegation looked unavoidable when Gage and Bitel had taken over so they couldn't be blamed for that. Nevertheless, the fans would be quick to judge if the Latics performed anywhere near as poorly the following season.

1993/94

Wigan Athletic fans must have had mixed emotions when Bitel announced his ambitions for the club at the start of the 1993/94.

"We looked at what Dario Gradi had done at Crewe and that was our model. We thought they were a club with a small ground, smallish crowds but with a good manager. They produced player after player and they consistently performed well in those days and were challenging to go up to the First Division. I wouldn't for one minute say we had aspirations to take Wigan Athletic to the Premiership. That wasn't thought possible. I don't think anyone could have imagined that would happen."

Having the Latics emulate Gradi's Crewe wasn't a new notion to the fans. It had been attempted during the Kenyon / Hamilton era. Though Hamilton had enjoyed enormous success in developing and selling talent, all the fans saw was the effects of the policy. Namely the deteriorating league form that resulted in relegation to the Endsleigh League Division Three.

Gage and Bitel would have their work cut out to persuade fans that the club could perform the balancing act as well as Crewe. It was a tough brief and that brief fell to Gradi's long time assistant at Crewe, Kenny Swain. The new owners were convinced he was the man for the job.

"Swain was a coach with a great reputation so we had every confidence in him," says Gage.

Only time would tell if Swain, who is now Head Coach of England Under-16s, was up to the challenge. Harold Ashurst remembers that this question was answered a lot quicker than anyone had expected. After six games in charge, the Latics, who had been relegated and should have been one of the better teams in the league, had not recorded a single win.

"We knew from the second game of the season that they were going to

Stephen Gage & Kenny Swain

finish way down the table. It was awful. The football was terrible. Swain had nothing to work with."

Alex Cribley echoes the view of Ashurst.

"When Swain joined as manager we only had about seven players on the books. He had to beg, borrow and steal everything."

A decent run in the FA Cup, where the Latics lost out by a single goal to Grimsby in the third round, could not mask the fact that the club seemed set on an unerring road to relegation. Relegation from Division Two was bad enough but relegation from Endsleigh League Division Three would mean non-league football at Springfield Park for the first time in 15 years. It was unthinkable and it was not the start that Gage and Bitel had wished for.

"We had high hopes when we hired Swain as manager but that turned out to be a very bad mistake," admits Bitel. "He was an excellent coach but his managerial credentials were clearly not there."

Gage shares the blame for Swain's poor start in management.

"Unfortunately he wasn't equipped with handling the senior players and we couldn't give him the time or the money to succeed."

It was true. Gage had steadied the ship but there wasn't any money available for Swain to bring in fresh blood. He and Bitel had taken on the club's liabilities and tidied up the business side but they didn't have massive amounts of cash to plough into the club. It would be a major contributing factor in the club ending the season nineteenth in the league. It was a terrible season but, with the club seemingly in free fall, escaping relegation was actually seen as a minor victory by the long-suffering fans.

The few fans that were still coming to watch the uninspired football on offer couldn't believe that the club had come so close to losing its hard-won League status. That surely would have been the end of the club as they knew it. They weren't sure how much more they could stomach. Swain would get one more chance to turn the team around but Gage and Bitel would be watching his every move. At the first sign of a slump the following season Swain would be out of the door. The last thing the club could take was a return to non-league. Its League status had to be protected at all costs.

Gage and Bitel soon found themselves in the same position as so many owners before them. They discovered that running a football club is not like running any other business. Things at the club weren't going to change overnight. For that to happen someone was going to have to come along with millions to spend.

"I remember in our first full season in charge I would go and see director, Stan Jackson, and the pair of us would raid our personal accounts to pay the players and staff," says Gage. "We were on a knife edge. Some Fridays I'd get a call from Brenda saying we didn't have enough money for the wages. I'd have a whip round with the other directors, people Jim Bennet, who was fantastic to the club. We never once failed to pay the players.

Sometimes we were getting just 1,000 for a home game

"A lot of clubs in the league couldn't say that. They'd sometimes borrow money off the PFA and not pay it back. We never got into the situation where we owed millions of pounds. It was just a case of not getting enough fans through the turnstiles to cover the costs. Sometimes we were getting just 1,000 for a home game. Those were the real die-hards, without whom the club would not be here today."

It was a similarly rude awakening for Bitel. The new vice-chairman shared Gage's frustration with the vagaries of running a football club.

"I admit that I made a miscalculation. I thought that football clubs could be run as businesses. But they can't. I thought I could bring tighter financial control and restructure things but ultimately, as happened to us, when you set out a budget for your manager for the season then your centre forward gets injured and you're languishing in the lower reaches of the table, that budget doesn't mean very much.

Above & Below:
Springfield Park

"Things at the club were very precarious still and the directors were putting their hands in their pockets to pay the wages because there weren't enough people coming through the turnstiles. Mind you the football on offer was not great. You couldn't just buy your way out of trouble though. You still needed some success on the pitch first to attract the better players. All in all the atmosphere around the football club was poor and the stadium was just not a good place to go and watch football."

The holy trinity, and indeed vicious circle of Poor Entertainment, Low Crowds and Decrepit Stadium, all played out against a context of crippling debt, would haunt Gage and Bitel as much as they had done all the club's previous owners. The only thing that the two felt they could change with some degree of certainty was the latter. A new stadium was seen as key to the club moving forward. Many of the fans had accepted it. Whether the plans that the two had would be as divisive as Kenyon's remained to be seen. Whether they'd be in control of the club long enough to see through those plans was another matter altogether.

8   TIME TO GROW

The first thing that had struck Stephen Gage and Nick Bitel when they'd taken over Wigan Athletic was that a stadium move was going to be key to regenerating the club. There was a possibility that the club might grow organically and, with a little success, attract the fans back but in reality until they boasted a modern stadium, one where it was a pleasure to watch football, as opposed to being a health and safety hazard, the club was stuck in the mire. Gage explains how a variety of plans were discussed, including a controversial move to ground share with the Latics' rugby league counterparts. It was a notion that put horror in the hearts of football fans in the town.

"The nub of the thing was that the club either needed to redevelop Springfield Park or move to a better site like Robin Park," says Gage. "Soon after I first took over the club I went to see Jack Robinson at Wigan Warriors. They were World Club Champions at the time and they weren't interested in any sort of cooperation with us at all. So we moved forward with our own plans. We hired Tony Stephens as a consultant. He'd later become David Beckham's agent. He'd done a good job on the new stadium at Huddersfield and he did a study that showed that a new stadium could work for a club of our size. We were talking about developing a community stadium with a capacity of 5-8,000. We had plans to build a ground that would have been right for The Championship, which we thought was realistic for the club."

Bitel was in full agreement about the stadium move. One thing he insisted that the pair would never have done, however, was take the club out of the town.

"We decided that was never going to happen while we were in charge. You can't move a club out of its heartland. People even thought it was disgraceful to try and move the club to Robin Park. I disagreed. Everyone recognised that for the club to be financially viable it would have to move away from Springfield Park. As long as you were there you would be having to put your hand in your pocket. We thought a stadium at Robin Park with some enabling development to help pay for it was the way forward. That way we'd get some income to help us with the shortfall. We started talks with the council and struggled on trying to do that for some time."

The mooted stadium move would never come to fruition under Gage and Bitel but the groundwork they did would prove invaluable when the club's next owner moved into the boardroom. He would prove that the pair's vision for a new stadium, shared with the rugby club was not such an outrageous idea after all.

If only the two forward-thinking owners could have as much influence on the park. With the season just weeks old Kenny Swain's time at the club was running out. After recording six losses and one solitary victory (in the League Cup) in their first seven games, the Latics were rock bottom in the Endsleigh League Division Three with no points. Swain was given his marching orders.

After Swain's dismissal, the man charged with turning the club's fortunes around was former Latics player Graham Barrow.

"They had no points on the board whatsoever having played six league games," says Barrow. "The club had got where it was because it had been selling its best players for years. The club ended up with average players, no points and heading toward the League exit door. It was drastic. With the exception of Ian Killford, Dave McKearney and Simon Palmer you could almost forget about the rest. That is how bad it had got. It was crisis time."

Barrow is right. The club was spiralling out of control despite the best efforts of Gage and Bitel. The crowds were terminally low. When the Latics hosted Aston Villa in the League Cup second round only 2,633 turned out to watch. Still, it was better than the 1,421 that had paid to see the club beat Crewe in the first round.

Graham Barrow

Barrow's arrival seemed to spark a mini revival at the club, however. He is a still held in high regard with fans for rescuing the club from almost certain relegation back to non-league. No-one was more relieved to see things turn around than Gage.

"Graham won his first game in charge and then we stuttered a bit and went on a run. It was grim but slowly things on the pitch improved, the crowds started slowly coming back and there was a feeling that the club was coming back to life. Graham had a knack of bringing in players and blending them into the team. He brought in players like Mark Leonard and Andy Farrell who added some much-needed experience."

So confident was Gage in the young manager's revolution that he made the foolhardy (considering the state of the club's finances) gesture of making money available for players. It is likely to have been the £40,000 proceeds of the sale of Phil Daley to Lincoln that funded the spending spree. Small fees were paid for Andy Lyons and David Miller while a weighty £20,000 and £12,500 were paid for Andy Farrell and Tony Black respectively. It wasn't much but the fans responded well to seeing some investment being made in the team for the first time in years.

With the club having climbed up to seventeenth in the table early in the year, Bitel even found some cause for optimism:

"Graham did a good job under a set of very difficult circumstances. He had virtually no money to spend and brought in some experienced, hard working players. He was an honest, decent manager. We started to think that with a couple of loans, a couple of decent buys, and a manager like Graham, that the club could start to do things. We could then move to Robin Park and have a viable club with the

We thought reaching The Championship was the sort of thing we could do

financial strength to go on from there. We thought that with a following wind, reaching The Championship one day was the sort of thing we could do."

Bitel's hopes in the New Year were in stark contrast with the despair that had greeted the start of the season. But now, with the team playing decent football for the first time in the Gage era, and the fans again trickling back to the terraces to witness Wigan's great escape, the atmosphere at the club was the best it had been for a decade. Barrow was one of the few that urged caution. With the club still languishing in the bottom half of the table nothing was decided. It had a long way to go to be freed from the financial burden that weighed the club down too. A trip to Altrincham for an FA Cup second round tie highlighted the tension that bubbled beneath the surface.

"Before we faced Altrincham, the draw for the next round had already been made," says Barrow. "We knew the winner would play Tottenham. The board had already made plans to smarten the ground with the proceeds from the Spurs match but we got beaten by Altrincham and you could tell how disappointed they were from the looks on their faces. Brenda Spencer was crying on the bus afterwards."

Bitel admits that the proceeds from the potential meeting with the top flight club had already been allocated.

"There were plans for what to do with the money from the next match against Spurs so we were all disappointed. Graham was too. I remember pulling him out of the referee's room after the match!"

Just as nothing could be taken for granted on the pitch, off it the club's financial problems were not going to just disappear because of a few good league results. Thanks to Gage, the club was no longer bleeding money. It just wasn't bringing in

Thanks to Gage, the club was no longer bleeding money

anywhere near enough revenue. It could not even rely on the usually lucrative Christmas fixtures – when good crowds could be expected – that season.

"We had a couple of games in a row cancelled for bad weather and we struggled. It was a massive set-back. We had no money coming in at all and people to pay. It was real hand to mouth stuff."

Gage and Bitel never doubted that taking over Wigan Athletic was going to be anything other than a challenge. They should take great credit from the fact that the club never went into administration like so many other clubs in the early 1990s. It was the easy option but the club had more principles than to leave their creditors high and dry. But Gage and Bitel must have started to question the endeavour that season when they discovered that the club's long time shirt sponsor was terminating the arrangement. It was one of the few bits of guaranteed revenue and the club relied on it.

The loss of Heinz's backing was a blow to the club but the desperate search for a replacement would bring Gage and Bitel into contact with a local businessman who just months later would become Wigan's white knight.

"Heinz was a fantastic sponsor but they came to me at the start of the season and said they weren't going to renew their sponsorship," says Gage.

Duncan Sharpe

"They were laying people off at the local factory and didn't want to be seen to be putting money into football when people were losing their jobs. With the loss of our main sponsor it didn't look good at all. We needed a miracle.

"We scratched our heads for a while because people weren't exactly queuing up to replace Heinz. Stan Jackson offered to contact Dave Whelan at JJB Sports to see if he wanted to be our shirt sponsor. Luckily he agreed and we all breathed a sigh of relief."

After signing on as shirt sponsor due, allegedly, in no small part to the insistence of his son-in-law Duncan Sharpe, who was a huge Latics fan, Whelan wasted no time in spelling out his long term intentions to Gage.

"The first time I met Whelan he said, 'One day when the time is right I'm going to buy this club from you. I'm going to merge it with the rugby club and put a super stadium up for Wigan.' He was quite matter-of-fact. I joked with him that the easiest of the three was to buy the club."

Come late February that season the club was still in the bottom half of the league. It was struggling to even pay the player's wages and Stan Jackson again turned to his old friend for help. Whelan claims not to have been able to refuse:

"When Wigan couldn't pay the players, Stan knocked on my door. He was clearly upset and said, 'I can't pay the wages'. I was out of football then but football was still in my blood and I'd had some fabulous years in game and had became quite a wealthy man from sport. I felt I had to help them out. I'd had so many good times in football, I had to put something back."

The one-off gesture didn't take long to transform into a deal to buy the club outright.

"I'm not sure what Stan's sales pitch was but far from paying the wages he ended up buying the whole club," recalls Bitel. "He paid us a small sum and paid off some of the club's debts. He turned up at the stadium on the first day and went straight out and cut the grass on the pitch."

But who was this mysterious figure who'd come to the rescue of his hometown club and how far did he expect to take them?

Dave Whelan is a Wiganer through and through. He was bred if not indeed born in the town. The two-up, two-down terraced house he grew up in is far removed from the palatial homes he boasts in places as far flung as Barbados. However it is from the modest house he shared with four siblings, mother and club singer/coal miner father that Whelan set out on the road to become one of the richest men in England, boasting a £200m fortune.

Business was to be Whelan's second choice career. As a promising footballer he played first for Wigan Boys Club before being signed by Blackburn Rovers at 17. The tough tackling right half spent a couple of seasons in the reserves before, according to Ian Halliwell, displaying a ruthless streak that would later serve him well in the corporate world.

"Back in 1956 Whelan played for the Blackburn Rovers reserves as a right half," says Halliwell. "His friend was the right back. At the time Whelan's father was the only person in their street that had a telephone and one morning the manager rang Dave Whelan and asked if he would pop round to his friend's house to ask him to report to the first team. Later that day Whelan turned up at the ground himself. He said he couldn't get in touch with his friend but the story goes that he'd never even tried."

One way or another Whelan broke into the Blackburn first team that season and never looked back. He enjoyed four good years with the club culminating in an FA Cup final appearance in 1960. At 23, Whelan had a glowing future in the game ahead of him. It was not to be, however. The final would end with Whelan suffering an horrific leg break and staring retirement from the game in the face. Whelan recalls the heartache it caused at the time.

"It was a sad blow, a bad blow for me. But I always thought I could play football again. I never gave up hope."

Whelan did play again but a second leg break soon after ended his football career for good. Newspaper feature writers

Far from being a mediocre footballer, Whelan was at the top of his game

often cite Whelan's unfulfilled football career as the thing which made him so driven to succeed in business. Saying so implies that his brief career in football wasn't quite as successful as Whelan's PR machine makes it out to be. Nothing could be further from the truth. Far from being a mediocre footballer, Whelan was at the top of his game when he broke his leg and was being tipped for an England call up.

Wigan legend, Les Campbell, has no doubt that Whelan had the talent to play at the very highest level:

"I played with Dave at Wigan Boys Club. He was a good player and when he went to Blackburn he played me out of the game quite a few times when I was with Preston. I've never said it to him but I think that if he hadn't broken his leg he would definitely have gone on to play for England."

We'll never know if that would have been the case. At 23, Whelan was on the scrap heap. Undeterred by the set-back Whelan used the £400 pay-off he got from Blackburn wisely and bought a grocery stall on Blackburn market. It wasn't the typical profession for an ex-footballer but Whelan enjoyed it and he worked every hour God sent to grow his business from just one stall to a chain of six supermarkets. In 1978, Whelan is thought to have sold his chain of Whelan Discount Stores to Wm Morrison for £1.5m.

No sooner had Whelan sold his supermarket chain than he turned his attention to a Wigan sports shop he had bought for a reported £7,400 in 1971. The JJB name is thought to originate from when rugby player JJ Broughton first opened the eponymous store in 1903. The store was later taken over by a JJ Braddock, only later, and unbelievably, to be bought by a certain JJ Bradburn. The name JJB stuck and when Whelan took over the store he probably couldn't have renamed the store even if he'd wanted to.

Whelan slowly changed the focus of JJB from fishing tackle and maggots to cut-price sportswear. Confident that he'd struck upon a winning formula, in the 1980s Whelan undertook one of the most aggressive expansions to hit the retail sector and soon there was a JJB Sports in almost every high street of every major town and city in the UK.

With an already massive personal fortune in 1989, Whelan almost bought Manchester United. If he had it is unlikely that Wigan Athletic as we know it would exist today. After Michael Knighton's failed attempt to buy the club, United approached Whelan to sound him out on the possibility of buying a 51 per cent stake in the club for £11m. Given United's current valuation in the region of £1bn, it is no wonder that Whelan was said in his own words to be, "very tempted." Whelan's plan hit the buffers when the implications of merging the football club with his JJB sportswear empire were explored.

"We discussed this at great length but when I came away from the meeting I had a thought," said Whelan in *The Times*. "JJB was spreading everywhere and I wondered whether Liverpool, Everton or Arsenal supporters would go into JJB stores if the company also owned Manchester United. I realised the idea would never work."

United weren't the only club that Whelan could have ploughed his considerable fortune into. Blackburn Rovers also courted the businessman before his close friend Jack Walker took over the club. It is thought that Walker's success at Blackburn inspired Whelan to try and do the same at Wigan Athletic.

Whelan's dalliances with the two clubs did not distract him from continuing to grow JJB. By 1994 there were 120 JJB stores in the UK and the company was floated with a valuation of £64.5m. It made Whelan a very, very rich man. It is no coincidence that the businessman took over Wigan Athletic soon after.

Today Whelan has taken a back seat at JJB to focus more attention on Wigan Athletic as its Premiership adventure continues. In addition to owning the Latics, Whelan also owns Wigan Warriors Rugby League Club (more of which later) and Orrell Rugby Union Club.

So Whelan is a Wigan man, a football man, and a man of considerable means. He seemed perfect for the club and what fans wanted to know more than anything else when he first arrived was what on God's earth did a man with such vast personal wealth have in mind for the club? Whelan wasted no time as in stating his ambitions.

"First and foremost my ambition with Wigan Athletic was to get into the Premiership within ten years," recalls Whelan. "To get there we needed to have a new stadium. If we were going to go to the top we had to have a ground to match. I was pretty sure we could get out of Division Three easily enough. It would be harder still to get into the Championship and harder still to get from there into the Premiership. But that was the ambition and I was prepared to work hard and spend the money to enable the club to achieve it."

Whelan's comments left some fans speechless. The Latics, in the Premiership? It was almost impossible to imagine even if the club spent all of Whelan's £200m fortune. Most fans know that money can't buy success and considering the club were still being watched by just 1,500 it seemed probable that any new stadium would end up being an expensive, empty white elephant. It wasn't only on the terraces that Whelan's ambitions were questioned. Brenda Spencer, who had been anointed the club's new chief executive by Whelan, never thought for one minute that the chairman's dreams would be realised.

"Dave said he was prepared to back the club to make them more successful. He also said he'd have us in the Premiership within ten years. We all laughed. My goal had always been to get the club to the Championship. I couldn't see us going further than that."

The takeover was a surprise for everyone at the club. The way the news was broken to staff was a bone of contention for Barrow:

"It was a shock when Whelan took over the club. The team were on a good run after getting out of trouble and there had been no hint of a change of ownership. I remember it was a Thursday morning and Gage said there was a meeting for all staff. When we all went up, Gage said, 'Meet your new owner', and introduced us to Whelan. I thought they might have given me some warning."

Whelan's coup mid-way through the 1994/95 season surprised and indeed confounded many in the town.

"People in Wigan thought Dave Whelan was mad to take over," recalls Harold Ashurst. "Still, it couldn't have been worse than what went before and people knew that had he not come in when he did, the club would probably be non-league again by now."

Having seen owners and directors at the club change as frequently as the seasons, some at the club weren't sure what to expect from their new employer.

"When Whelan took over we were close to going out of business," says Alex Cribley. "It looked bleak. We were near the bottom of the Football League and there didn't seem to be any way out of it because we couldn't afford to buy any decent players. When Dave came onboard we didn't immediately think that all our problems had been solved. We knew he'd agreed to take on the club's debt but no-one was sure what to expect beyond that."

Whelan's investment brought a two year adventure to an end for Gage and Bitel. Gage remained on the board at the request of Whelan. Bitel resigned his position but left with no regrets.

"I wouldn't say we were a great success but we took over a club that was going under and steadied it. We always knew there was going to be a gap in the funding and we recognised quite quickly that we would struggle with the club for a number of reasons. Not least because neither Stephen or I lived in Wigan, or were from there."

Barrow, has nothing but respect for what the pair achieved in their time at the club.

"Stephen and Nick made every effort to make things right. They did what they could in the face of paltry crowds on the terraces and always had the best interests of the club at heart right up to the very end."

Barrow would be the first but by no means the last Latics manager under Dave Whelan. With the season mid-way through, he would hope that his job was secure until at least the end of the season, especially in light of the miracles he'd worked to stave off the threat of relegation. His first impressions of the new owner were good.

"My first experience of Whelan was very positive. He changed my club car from a second hand Ford Granada to a new Mercedes. There was a slight improvement on my contract and there was talk of sorting out the pitch. It was all football-based and there was nothing negative about it at all. It was a breath of fresh air to have someone talking about spending £20,000 on the pitch. We went to look at Bolton's training ground with a view to buying it too. It was exactly what you wanted to hear from a new chairman and I was looking forward to a long and fruitful relationship."

Whelan was installed as chairman in time for the club's home game against Hartlepool United on February 28, 1995. A 2-0 victory boded well for Barrow's short term future at the club and it saw the club climb to twelfth in the table. The paltry crowd of 1,452 who watched that day told Whelan everything he needed to know about the task in hand.

Whelan's next act as chairman gave out more good signals to Barrow.

"After I'd signed my new contract Whelan said, 'You're off to Spain to look at a few players'. Up until then I'd been watching non-league sides and Liverpool and Manchester United reserves for new players. I flew to Zaragoza and went into the middle of nowhere to watch two players. A third had a video of himself which I had a look at. I came back the next day and the chairman asked me what I thought. I told him that they were more than useful and that it would be great to get them over. Isidro Diaz, Jesus Seba and Roberto Martinez, the 'Three Amigos' as they would become known, arrived the following week and it was JJB all over. Whelan had outlets in Spain so the publicity didn't do his company any harm. He said to me afterwards: 'It costs

Isidro Diaz, one of the Three Amigos, Wigan v Lincoln, 23rd December 1995

an absolute fortune to advertise on TV but I got all the publicity I wanted from the signings and, most importantly, we've got three good players'."

Wigan's poor start to the season put paid to any promotion or play-off aspirations that season and they'd end the campaign a respectable fourteenth in the table. Barrow had truly stopped the rot, however, and was looking forward to rebuilding the squad in anticipation of their first full campaign under new ownership. Despite Whelan's considerable wealth the club did not immediately go on a spending spree. It actually recorded a £7,500 profit from the transfer market at the end of Whelan's first season. Whelan was biding his time before letting Barrow spend his money. It was a fact the manager was acutely aware of and it made him worry for his future at the club.

"At the end of the season I requested a meeting with Whelan. We'd ended the season well. The team spirit had returned to the dressing room and people were coming back to watch us because we were playing good football. I didn't think we'd need that much investment in the club to get out of that league the next season so I wanted to know where I stood. I took the bull by the horns. I went to see Whelan and said, 'You've bought the club. I think I'm the man for this job but if you're not comfortable with it I'm prepared to step aside, shake hands and wish you the best of luck for the future.' Straight away he said, 'No, no, no'. He offered me a 12 month rolling contract on the spot.

"I was pleased to have his backing but it was a bizarre time. I was getting calls from some big names in football, like Ron Atkinson, telling me what a great opportunity it was and how much money I had to spend. But I was never once told that by the chairman."

It was obvious that Whelan was going to have to open his wallet sooner or later. In the eyes of the fans, and indeed many of the staff at the club, Barrow had done more than enough to earn the right to be the man to rebuild the team. Despite this, and having been given the word of the new chairman, the young manager couldn't shake the feeling that his days were numbered.

9   LOFTY AMBITIONS

Dave Whelan's first full season at the club was the most hotly anticipated since the Latics had kicked off the 1985/86 season as freshly crowned Freight Rover Trophy champions and favourites for promotion. Following the signing of the Three Amigos and his outlandish claims that he intended to take the club all the way to the top, the fans didn't know what to expect next from their new owner.

With talk of Whelan's lofty ambitions ringing in his ears Graham Barrow must have felt no small degree of pressure as he prepared for the 1995/96 season. The Premiership was a long way away, light years in most peoples' eyes, but Barrow knew there would be great expectation that the long journey should start with one small step out of the bottom tier of the Football League that very season.

Barrow was ready for the challenge but until the chairman gave him the green light to strengthen the squad his hands were tied. The Latics didn't get off to the perfect start. A loss away to Gillingham on the opening day of the season was followed by defeat by Chester City in the second round of the League Cup. The Latics recorded a much-needed home win in the league in their next fixture but the very next game they lost to Chester in the League Cup second leg in front of just 2,061 fans. Whelan's revolution was getting off to the quietest of starts.

Barrow's side were, however, playing some of the best football the club had played since the likes of Newell, Jewell, Lowe, Langley, and indeed Barrow had graced the team. Having brought in John Pender, who joined for £30,000 from Burnley as his first signing, Whelan loosened the purse strings further for Barrow on September 9, 1995. Colin Greenhall's arrival from Lincoln for £45,000 was seen as a shrewd bit of business. Wigan-born Greenhall and Pender added a bit of much-needed muscle at the back and they would go on to become a mainstay of the team in seasons to come. Barrow was convinced that the two would be the first of many signings as the club geared up for a promotion push. The Latics were sitting thirteenth in the league when Greenhall joined. Little did Barrow know that he had only seven games left as Wigan Athletic manager. He was about to become the first Latics manager to be sacked by the new chairman. In time Barrow would see that the 'Ex-Wigan Athletic Managers, 1995-present Club' would not be an exclusive one.

In the run up to Barrow's last game, a 6-2 thrashing at the hands of Mansfield Town on October 7, the Latics won once, drew three times and lost twice in the league. It wasn't the best league record but it wasn't the worse either. Going into the clash at Springfield Park, Wigan were still thirteenth in the table, five places above Mansfield. The Latics were just three points off fifth place and as it was early in the season there were certainly no alarm bells ringing. Barrow's

Barrow's time as manager came to an unceremonious end

team continued to play good, if not always winning, football. Yet two days after the Mansfield defeat, Barrow's time as Latics manager came to an unceremonious end.

Barrow was confounded and hurt by the decision:

"It was a total shock to be sacked. The first I knew about it was on the Sunday when I was informed to clear my desk and that I'd be having a meeting with the chairman during the week. Everyone I knew in the game was genuinely taken aback. It was a shock to the players too. As far as I was concerned the chairman had backed me at the start of the season and given me a new contract. I think that for all his business experience and his football experience, which I thought was going to be a big plus, that he might have been a bit more patient.

"About ten days after I'd been sacked Whelan found time to see me. The only thing that might have precipitated the sacking was the fact that we'd been beaten 6-2 by Mansfield Town. We were 3-2 down and I made a tactical change, going to three at the back. I thought maybe we could get something out of the game or worse case scenario we'd lose another goal. As we were behind already there was nothing to lose. But Whelan never asked my why I'd done it.

"When I left we were just outside the play-offs with a new squad, we were playing good football, creating lots of chances and I had the full backing of the fans. I'd had some money to spend. I'd just brought in what I considered to be the backbone of the team in Greenhall and Pender but I was only given two games with them. Not to get until Christmas was harsh. It was the biggest

John Deehan

kick in the teeth I've had in football to be honest.

"If you ask any of the players who were there at the time they'll tell you that we were on the right track. I knew we were too. Very rarely in football will a manager call you up and thank you for the squad you have left him but that is exactly what my successor John Deehan did, so I knew I must have been doing something right. John brought some more players in but the two centre halves especially would help the club get out of that league eventually. That was always going to be a possibility if the manager was given enough money to spend."

A lot of fans and people in the game thought that Barrow should have been given longer to prove himself, especially in light of how he'd saved the club from relegation the season before. The fact that Whelan never gave Barrow an explanation for his sacking only made it worse.

With the season in full flight Frank Lord stepped immediately into the void and the result was a morale boosting 4-0 win at Exeter. Lord's time in the hot seat would be short-lived. Whelan wasted no time in contacting John Deehan who had just left Premiership Norwich City about the job.

"Initially I was invited up to meet Dave," says Deehan. "We sat for an hour and I explained my ideas and I think with him being a businessman he'd seen that I had a long term plan for the team. I laid out my plans and ideas and said this is my plan, this is how I operate and this is how I expect it to work. I told him where I expected to be after a couple of years which was in Division Two. I think that was what got me the job. There were some big names in for it but I'd done my groundwork and I knew what it was going to take to bring success to the club because I'd just managed in the Premiership. Whelan hired me soon after. Unusually I was never asked to sign a contract but Whelan seemed quite comfortable with the situation."

The main difference between Deehan and Barrow was that Deehan was Whelan's man. Thus, Whelan gave Deehan a virtually open chequebook to build a squad to take the team out of Division Three. Luckily for Deehan, he spent wisely.

"I didn't realise how wealthy Whelan was when I joined. He said to me, 'If you need a little bit of money it will be made available to you.' Kevin Sharp was the first player I signed, at the end of November 1995. He came from Leeds for £50,000. He was a long term acquisition for the club. He and Gavin Johnson played on the left. Both of them could have been playing two leagues higher up.

"I had a real simple plan. We had to get a rod of steel through the middle of the team. We brought in Graeme Jones up front. We brought in Lee Butler in goal. I was very happy with the centre backs. Greenhall and Pender were great players. I added people like Neil Rimmer and later Paul Rogers to help Roberto Martinez. We had a good solid team with strength down the middle. We had Johnson and Sharp on the left and Izzy Diaz on the right who was spectacular for us."

Deehan's team finished the season in tenth place, only narrowly missing out on a play off place after an end of season defeat to Northampton. It was the third loss on the trot for the Latics and while some fans felt that not reaching the play offs was a failure. Deehan was disappointed but pragmatic:

"When I came in I wanted us to get out of the league as soon as possible. In hindsight, if we had gone up that season we might not have been ready."

A decent FA Cup run saw the club reach the third round that season and brought fans some comfort. As better players began to sign for the club and the football on offer continued to improve, so too did the crowds. 3,224 turned out to watch the Latics beat Runcorn in the FA Cup first round replay in late November. It doesn't sound like much but it was more than double what a typical gate had been just a season or so before for what could hardly be described as a glamour tie.

Transition is a word that has become synonymous with Whelan's early years at Wigan Athletic but that is exactly what the 1995/96 season was. Whelan was growing impatient for that first vital promotion, however. The fans just wanted a sign that would tell them if Whelan really was the fairy godmother they'd waited an eternity for. Then, and only then, would they buy into Whelan's outlandish dream that Wigan Athletic could one day be a force to be reckoned with in the Premiership.

By the time David Lowe rejoined the Latics late in the 1995/96 season for a then record £125,000, the club was already changing out of all recognition behind the scenes. It bore no resemblance to the ramshackle outfit that Lowe had left behind for Ipswich nine years before. Whelan was beginning to pump money into the club in all the areas that had been neglected under previous chairmen.

"When Deehan took me back to Wigan the Whelan era had just begun," recalls Lowe. "There was a training ground, which we'd never had before, the plans for the new stadium were starting to take shape and everything was moving in the right direction. It was the start of the rebuilding process and it was great to be involved, especially knowing how bad things had been for the club before."

1996/97

Lowe wasn't the only new signing that Deehan brought in to bolster the squad for the 1996/97 season. In preparation for his first full tilt at promotion he brought in Andy Saville from Preston North End (£100,000), Paul Rogers from Notts County (£50,000), Roy Carroll from Hull City (£350,000), and Scott Green and David Lee from Bolton (£300,000 and £250,000 respectively). It brought Deehan's spending to the better part of £1.5m. With every new player the fans' astonishment grew. They'd never seen a spending spree like it and slowly they started to back the Whelan revolution.

Having spent so much money, particularly for a Nationwide League Division Three team, Deehan knew expectations would be high that season. Latics fans had learnt long ago to have low expectations in the league but Deehan knew that they'd soon learn how to change that. If Deehan were to be judged on the cup competitions that year he probably would have followed Barrow out of the exit door quicker than you could say Roberto Martinez, who starred for the team that season. The Latics went out of the FA Cup in the first round to Blackpool, out of the AutoWindscreens Shield to a Shrewsbury Town golden goal, and out of the League Cup 7-6 on aggregate to Preston in the first round.

What was significant about the latter tie was that 3,713 fans turned out to watch the Latics. Again, it was not a massive crowd but if you compare it to the 2,061 the corresponding cup tie attracted to Springfield Park in the 1995/96 season or the 1,421 that watched the League Cup first round match against Crewe in the 1994/95 season, it was a great leap forward. It would still not cover the bills, especially the wage bill now that the club had made some big signings – Whelan was now picking that up – though he did aim to make the club self financing one day. He knew that getting the crowds back to Springfield Park, and indeed the club's new stadium when it was built, was key to the long term survival of the club. Whelan was mooting building a 25,000 seater stadium in Robin Park so the breadth of his ambition was there for all to see. It was also apparent

John Deehan celebrating Wigan Athletic's promotion to the Second Division

for all to see that he was building a stadium to be used in a league higher that the one the club found itself in 1996/97.

With no cup competitions to distract Deehan's squad they set about trying to win promotion for the club for the first time since 1982. The season is best summarised by the man who was in the manager's hot seat.

"That season there were two dominant teams in the league – ourselves and Fulham," says Deehan. "We had some brilliant results during the campaign and were soon at the top of the league. We beat Scarborough 7-1, which was a record win in the league for the club with Lowe and Diaz both scoring twice. We were on fire that night. We secured promotion with about six or seven games left in the season, we were that far clear. It was the target I had set out when I'd been interviewed for the job so I was particularly pleased. Whether we'd win the title would go down to the wire, however. Fulham were still breathing down our necks as the season-end neared."

It was a great achievement for the club to have won promotion. It meant everything to the long suffering staff. They knew that hard work had played just as important a part in the promotion as Whelan's money. Other clubs in

*Chairman Dave Whelan
with the Third Division Trophy*

the league taunted the Latics about their new 'moneybags' tag — only at away games mind. Any visitors to Springfield Park would have found it impossible to reconcile the reputation with the tumbledown stadium.

Knowing how the club had struggled in the past, Deehan was desperate to deliver the championship to the Lancashire club.

"Going into the last game of the season we still had Fulham on our tail. We were level on points so the championship was there for the taking. We were playing Mansfield Town at home needing to win to clinch the title. It was nil-nil at half time. I remember when I walked back out Dave Crompton, my youth team coach, was sat at the end of the tunnel with his head in his hands. I looked at him and I could see something in his eyes. I said, 'Fulham are winning aren't they?' He just nodded his head. That result would have made Fulham champions. I said to him, 'We'll get a goal here Dave. Keep faith with us'.

"We did score and ran out 2-0 winners through goals from Graham Lancashire and David Lowe. It still ranks as one of the best days of my footballing life. A lot of the lads in the team had never actually won a medal so it was a great day for them too. I'm very proud of that championship medal and I hope they are too. It was a wonderful day, a great result. I remember doing a lap of honour and my five-year-old son was walking with me. The crowd started coming onto the pitch and I lost him and panicked for a second. Then he appeared on a supporter's shoulders. It was fantastic. To see the joy and elation on the faces of the fans was great. People were laughing and screaming. Grown men were weeping openly. It was a very emotional day. It meant so much to them. They deserved it after what they had been through and there was a huge, huge party that night that went on for a very long time.

"It also meant a lot to people like Brenda Spencer, Stan Jackson and Alex Cribley – fantastic folk who were the heartbeat of the club, and not least Dave Whelan. He knew the players had given everything that season. They were a very good team and I was very proud to have been in charge of them. I can assure you that Whelan enjoyed winning the Division Three title every bit as much as winning The Championship in 2005."

It was a memorable season for Wigan Athletic. It was their first step on a dizzying journey up the leagues. The good times were back at the club and fans were voting with their feet too. Springy was sold out more than once that season. It was a sight to behold.

"We were selling out Springfield Park towards the end of the championship winning season," says Deehan. "It was great to see people hanging over that white wall behind the goal. It wasn't thought possible even one season before."

The hardcore of 1,500 who had stood by the club through thick and thin chided the fair-weather fans who started flooding back to watch the Latics. Deep down they knew they were exactly the people that had to keep coming to the club if they were ever going to keep up with Whelan's plans to put Wigan Athletic firmly on the football map.

1997/98

John Deehan, who was about to embark on his third season at the club, was taking on the look of a permanent fixture compared to previous managers. Deehan's management pedigree had taken a boost from winning the Third Division title and as the Latics prepared for their first spell in Division Two since 1993 an attempt was made to poach him away from the club.

"At the start of the 1997/98 season Stockport County asked if I'd be interested in becoming their manager. I always got on well with Whelan so I went and told him about the offer. I also told him that I believed that there was more potential at Wigan. He agreed and increased my salary to match the Stockport offer but I still didn't get a permanent contract."

Whelan's reluctance to give out permanent contracts to managers would characterise the next four years at the club, during which time no less than five more managers would occupy the management hot seat. Only the latter of these five would be offered a contract.

The Latics continued their faltering League Cup form when the 1997/98 season got underway and by August 26, 1997 they were out of the competition after losing to Chesterfield. The AutoWindscreens Trophy didn't provide any comfort either. They were knocked out of that in the Northern Quarter Final by Blackpool. The FA Cup provided the highlight of the three cup competitions in the 1997/98 season. The Latics disposed of Carlisle United in the first round before beating York City 2-1 at Springfield Park in the second in front of over 4,000 people. The club's reward was an away tie against Blackburn Rovers.

It was a great opportunity for the club to set out its stall but though the fans were gradually returning to Springfield Park, an indication of how far it still had to go can be gleaned from a conversation reputed to have been had by Whelan and Spencer after the FA Cup draw was made. On being allocated 5,000 tickets for the tie at Ewood Park, Brenda Spencer is said to have turned to the chairman and said, "How are we going to sell 5,000 tickets Dave? We only get 3,000 at home!"

The Latics almost caused an upset that day, eventually going down 4-2 to the Premiership side in an entertaining clash. 22,402 turned out to watch so the Latics must have sold at least some of its 5,000 tickets.

League form was not so good that season. John Deehan had brought in some more new faces including Pat McGibbon from Man Utd for £250,000

Football is such a precarious occupation, especially as a manager

and Brendan O'Connell from Charlton for £120,000 but the Nationwide League Division Two was a real step up for many of the players. A 5-2 thrashing of Wycombe Wanderers on the opening day of the season was not going to be emblematic of things to come. The Latics only won seven of their next 22 matches and by Boxing Day were just sixteenth in the table. After winning just four from the next fifteen by March 28, 1998 the club were lying in eighteenth place, just four points above the relegation zone. Knowing deep down that his squad was not up to the rigours of Division Two football, Deehan went to Whelan to ask for funds to bring in more quality. The chairman's response would be the first warning sign that Deehan was living on borrowed time.

"Whelan is a very demanding man but also a very honest and open man," says Deehan. "When I asked for money for a striker he told me that I'd had enough money to spend and that I had to work with the group I had. I knew they weren't going to be good enough to get out of that division, or to play in the next league up for that matter."

Whelan is a very demanding man but also a very honest and open man

With his hands tied, Deehan made the most of what he had and roused the squad to finish the season strongly. After the 1-1 draw with Preston in late March that put them eighteenth in the league, Deehan's team won five, drew two and lost just one match in the run in to finish a respectable eleventh, just a few points shy of the play-off places.

In the close season Whelan stood firm and didn't make any more money available to Deehan to bring in the players the manager thought the club so desperately needed. Deehan persevered, however, and was at the training ground preparing for another campaign when he received an interesting offer that would spell the end of his time at the club.

"It was getting near the start of the 1998/99 season when I took a call asking if I'd like to join Steve Bruce at Sheffield United. Sir Alex Ferguson was due to retire from Manchester United the following year and with Bruce touted as a possible successor you could envisage anything happening. I was interested but I wanted to be open with the chairman about it so I went to see him to see if there was a contract on offer for me from the club. He said there wasn't but that he wanted me to continue on a non-contract basis. That, along with his reluctance to let me bring in new players, basically told me that he'd prefer for me to move on. Football is such a precarious occupation, especially as a manager, and I'd got to the stage where I needed some sort of security. I decided to leave because I had always wanted to work with Steve Bruce but also to secure my family's future.

"When I look back I'd done my time at the club and I was very proud of what I'd achieved. I'd taken them up a division which is what I'd set out to do. They had held their own in Division Two too and had finished a creditable eleventh to consolidate their place in the league. Maybe it was time for a new manager to come in. I'm led to believe that JJB staff stay for ten months. I'd stayed for two and half years so I hadn't done badly. When I left I think there was a bit of turmoil at the club. They were desperate for someone to come in and take them up to the next division. The potential was there, it was just a case of finding the right person who could come in and do that."

Deehan's assessment is right. His leaving would see a period of instability at the club that would hinder its progress and frustrate the fans. After a promising start under Deehan, not until 2001 would Whelan's dream get properly back on track. In the interim the club would suffer some spectacular promotion near misses. During that time some of the biggest names in football would come through the door and be swiftly ushered out of it by Whelan. The last thing the fans had expected the multimillionaire to install at Springfield Park before it was demolished was a revolving door.

10　A MOST INTERESTING JOB

John Deehan's departure in the close season left one of the most interesting jobs in English football up for grabs. Whelan had told the world that Wigan Athletic were bound for the Premiership and any number of managers wanted to get a piece of the action.

The 1998/99 season would be Wigan Athletic's last at Springfield Park after a rocky 67 year tenure. Construction work had already started on the state of the art 25,000 seater JJB Stadium at Robin Park. The club would move there at the start of the following season to ground share with Wigan Warriors RLFC. With Whelan having rescued the rugby club from the brink too, it was inevitable that he would fulfil the dream he'd outlined to Gage many years before. He'd bought the Latics, bought the Warriors – now all he had to do was provide the people of Wigan with the 'super' stadium.

Fittingly, the Latics would be managed by one of their all time cult figures for their final season at Springy. Ray Mathias had taken over Bryan Hamilton's Freight Rover Trophy winning team in 1986 just as it was being sold off to save the club. Despite that, Mathias led the club to fourth place in the league and to an historic FA Cup quarter final with Leeds. The match will be remembered as one of the greatest matches ever held at Springfield Park.

The Wigan job was a great opportunity for Mathias and it was only a chance encounter with director, John Winstanley, which led to him being hired.

"I went to a pre-season game at the end of July where I bumped into John. We got chatting and I asked who was going to be the Latics' next manager. He told me they had interviewed a lot of people, including Ian Rush, but that the job hadn't been taken. He asked jokingly if I'd be interested. I'd just signed a three year contract at Tranmere but was definitely keen.

"John mentioned it to Whelan. I met with him first and we talked for an hour. He said he wanted to take the club to the Premiership. He made no bones about it. He told me that there was money there if I needed it. I met with the other directors and got the job a few days later. I started two days before the season began on August 3, 1998."

Like Deehan before him, Mathias was not offered a long term contract, rather a rolling week-to-week deal. He'd hit it off with Whelan and there was no reason to suggest he wouldn't be given a fair crack of the whip. It was the potential at Wigan that had drawn the ex-manager back to the club.

"The possibilities at Wigan were there for all to see. I was sure that I could get the team to show some progression that year even though I didn't get chance to work with the players at all during pre-season. When I was offered the job I asked Director of Football John Benson when I should start. It was 9am on Thursday and the first match was Saturday. 'Now!' he said. I was there within the hour and there was already kit laid out for me. It was a fantastic feeling to be back."

Mathias had the briefest of time to assess his squad and picked a similar team to the one he'd watched in pre-season for the Latics's first league match against Millwall. Unsurprisingly Wigan were well beaten. Mathias' second match in charge threw up an interesting grudge match. Graham Barrow travelled to Springfield Park with his Rochdale side for a League Cup first round tie. It would be Mathias' first win since his return. The Latics would go on to meet Norwich in the second round but, never having had a great record in the competition, fans weren't surprised to see the Latics go out against superior opposition. As Wigan's league status would change in the coming years so too would its League Cup credentials, however.

With the Latics sitting seventeenth in the league in early October after a shaky start, Mathias knew it was time to ring the changes.

"I introduced some new players because I didn't think the current squad was capable of winning promotion. As time went by I identified certain positions that needed strengthening. Whelan made money available to me to bring in new players. He was good to his word and I couldn't fault him for that. I signed Wales Under 21 international Simon Haworth for £600,000 from Coventry. I also signed Andy Liddell for £350,000."

Liddell's signing was perhaps Mathias' greatest legacy. He would prove to be one of the best players for the Latics over the next five years and led the team all the way to the Championship. To sign a player of that ability for that price was shrewd business. As Mathias says:

"Liddell was a dream of a player. He worked his socks off too and the fans loved him for it."

The October signings sparked a mini revival in the league and after beating a decent Reading side 1-0 on November 11, Mathias' men climbed to twelfth spot, just five points shy of the play-off positions. The Latics' next fixture was a home tie in the first round of the FA Cup against Blackpool. The visitors were dispatched 4-3 in a thrilling encounter watched by 4,640. If you compare that to the 4,021 that watched the Latics beat York City in the competition the season before, you can see that modest progress on building the fanbase, driven by Brenda Spencer at the behest of Whelan, was being made.

Wigan's FA Cup adventure would be ended in the second round when Notts County beat them on penalties after a replay. By this time the team was in the midst

David Lowe receiving the Player of the Year Award, 1998 from chairman Dave Whelan

of an eight match unbeaten run in the league that would see them climb to eighth in the table by New Year. Whelan began to sense that another promotion, one he so badly craved for his football club, was imminent. So much so that in the AutoWindscreens Shield that season he suggested that Mathias rest key players. Mathias was happy to oblige but soon it became apparent that the Latics were in with a great chance of winning the trophy for a second time.

"The chairman would say to me, 'We don't want to play our strongest side in this match', or, 'We don't actually want to win this game'," says Mathias. "He wanted to concentrate of the league. We had a good squad then. We played Rotherham who were doing well in Division Three. We made seven changes but we still won 3-0. We did the same against Carlisle in the next round. When the possibility of going to Wembley started to look likely the players all wanted to put themselves in contention for the final. The chairman changed his tune too."

Despite his reputation for getting involved in football matters, Whelan is more hands off than most club owners. The difference between your archetypal chairman and Whelan is that he used to play the game at the highest level. As Mathias explains, however, his relationship with Whelan was like that between any other manager and chairman.

"There have always been rumours that Whelan likes to get involved in the football side. He never did with me. Sometimes he'd call and ask why I wasn't playing a certain player and I'd give him a reason and he'd accept it. That was the end of it. I'd call him on a Friday to tell him what the team was going to be on Saturday but that is procedure at most clubs."

Whelan was right about resting players for the league run in. The AutoWindscreens Shield run did affect the Latics' league programme. They drew Carlisle in the Northern Quarter Final and the game got called off four times. By the end of the season the club would be left having to play seven games in 15 days in order to clinch a play-off place.

Still, beggars can't be choosers and Mathias' team went on to beat Rochdale 2-0 and Wrexham 5-2 on aggregate in the AutoWindscreens Shield Northern Final to seal a place in the Wembley final with Millwall. The Latics only conceded two goals en-route to that final. Mathias remembers the pride he felt leading the team out at Wembley:

"We took about 12,000 fans to London. There were about 55,000 inside Wembley that day so the noise was deafening. Having been at the club in the late 1980s I knew what the fans had been through. I knew what it would mean to them to win a trophy. I tried to instill this in the players. But Millwall had a decent team − a few of their players that day went on to play in the Premiership. They'd beaten us home and away in the league that year as well. It was a nervy encounter but we fought hard and won 1-0 through a last minute Paul Rogers goal. It couldn't have been more tense. There were wild celebrations by the players and the fans. I was delighted for every last one of them."

Mathias will long be remembered in Wigan for what he achieved with the Latics but there was nothing he wanted more than delivering promotion to the club in its final season at Springfield Park. The end of season run in was one of the most hectic and tense in Latics' history.

"We had to play seven games in 15 days in the run up to the play-offs," says Mathias. "At that time we didn't do any training because the players were either playing or travelling to the next game. We were chasing a couple of clubs and finally got into the play-offs by beating Chesterfield at home on the last day of the season.

"We'd played away at Wycombe on the Wednesday so the team were absolutely shattered before the match had even kicked off. We went a goal down and I remember thinking that we'd had it. All credit to the boys, though, we came back and won 3-1. We gave the players a rest after that having won four, drawn two and lost one of the seven matches. It was a fantastic achievement to qualify for the play-offs."

Mathias' squad had a week off to rest and ponder their play-off semi final match with Manchester City. The first leg would be the last competitive match to be played at Springfield Park and the Latics would have their work cut out to overcome a City side that had beaten them twice already in the league that season.

"We had some bad luck going into the play-offs," recalls Mathias. "Michael O'Neill was suspended and we had a few injuries to key players like Haworth and Liddell. Graeme Jones had been struggling with an injury and I had to choose between playing him or Lowe, who was coming to the end of his career, up front. We had to give Jones an injection in his ankle to even put him in contention. A couple of other players were also carrying knocks so I didn't want to risk another one, so I played Lowe.

The Latics celebrate winning the 1999 AutoWindscreens Shield

"We drew 1-1 in the first leg but we could have won it. Jones came off the bench for us and shook Man City up and was unfortunate not to score. It would have been good to give the old stadium a winning send off but it was not to be."

6,762 – a virtual full house – turned out to watch the Latics that day in the emotional encounter. The club would need them and a lot more if they were ever going to fill their new stadium. And it would be Second Division football that would be played at the new stadium the following season: City beat the Latics in the return leg in controversial style at Maine Road.

"We had a blatant penalty turned down and Shaun Goater scored a dubious goal," says Mathias. "The replay showed that he'd knocked it in with his arm. We should have won that game with the number of chances we missed."

It wasn't to be for Mathias and his team. The fans weren't displeased with a season that had seen the club lift a rare piece of silverware, narrowly lose in the play-offs and play such good football. Mathias was happy too.

"What we achieved that season was tremendous. There was massive progression. We finished sixth, got into the play-offs and won a trophy at Wembley. I was proud of what the team achieved. I couldn't compliment the players enough."

There was every reason for optimism. When the chairman announced that

The last league game at Springfield Park. Wigan players celebrate reaching the play-offs

the club was taking the management and players on holiday to reward them for their good season it seemed like he was content too. What was to happen next was to come as a surprise to everyone.

"We gave the players a couple of days off and arranged to meet back at the training ground to discuss the plans for the trip," says Mathias. "It was a gesture to show that we appreciated their efforts that season. When I arrived at the training ground Whelan was already there. I could sense something wasn't right. It was eerie. I spoke to him when I arrived and then an hour later he asked me to go for a chat. He said, 'I'm relieving you of your duties'. That was it. It was one of the biggest shocks I'd had in my life.

"After I was sacked I went and had a very emotional chat with the squad. We'd been through so much together that season. They were utterly shocked. Later I tried to call each of them up and thank them for what they had done for me. We all knew that the chairman wanted to climb up the leagues as quickly as possible and everyone had tried their hardest that season.

"The local press seemed as flabbergasted at the news of my sacking as I was. The only inkling of it I had was a few days before the play-off second leg. There was an article in the local paper where the chairman had apparently gone on record saying that if we didn't beat City I'd be out of a job. But I'd challenged the chairman about it already and he denied saying it."

In the days after his shock dismissal, Mathias searched for reasons as to why Whelan might have acted how he did.

"I knew that I couldn't achieve success at the club overnight. The first season I planned to sort the players out. If I'd got promotion that first year we would have had to be brilliant and have had a lot of luck. The second year I thought we should have been in or around the top three. With the players we had and those we would have been able to bring in we definitely would have got promoted.

"Looking back there was one area that I should have strengthened in the team. But the player who played there, who I won't mention, started playing really well. I decided not to upset the team because it had started gelling and I didn't think the disruption of bringing someone in would help."

Harold Ashurst who was by now working as a summariser on *WISH FM* recalls that Mathias' sacking came completely out of left field. His recollection of events sheds some light on Whelan's motives too.

"Ray had done really well since replacing Deehan. I spoke to him the day he was going to meet the chairman. He thought he was going to get a pay rise but he came out with his P45. The chairman told him he hadn't achieved what he'd been expected to achieve and he wasn't the man to take the club forward."

With Mathias out of the picture, Whelan had now gone through three managers in four years at the club. The fans, who had expected a new era of stability in the dressing room to match that in the boardroom, were starting to lose faith in Whelan's vision. The uneasy truce with the benefactor who had the means to fulfil the club's wildest ambitions was beginning to creak. Sacking the popular Mathias hadn't helped. If Whelan was to earn anywhere near the same amount of affection from the Latics faithful he'd have to learn to be more patient with his managers.

1999/2000

Only in the 1999/00 season could fans get a glimpse of the true ambition that owner Whelan had for the club. Wigan Athletic were about to be reborn in their new home. The JJB Stadium – bank-rolled by Whelan at a cost of £30m – would arm the Lancashire club with a vital weapon as it sought to grow. Namely, a 25,000 stadium replete with bars, executive boxes, conference facilities and last but by no means least Rigalettos, an on-site Italian restaurant named in honour of Whelan's club singer father 'Tony Rigaletto'.

The stadium, which was controversially to be shared with the Wigan Warriors, was officially opened with a football match on August 4, 1999. After hosting European champions Manchester United, much to the chagrin of rugby fans in the town, the stadium will forever be known as a football stadium where the rugby team plays. Warriors, also owned by Whelan, only moved to the stadium toward the end of their season and played there first on September 19, 1999.

The move to the JJB was a dream come true for many fans and staff at the club. Not everyone was sad to see Springfield Park redeveloped as housing. It could have been worse. Warriors' Central Park, where Whelan had initially wanted to build a new stadium for both clubs, would rather less grandly become the site for a supermarket. Former club chairman Stephen Gage is one man who will always have a soft spot for Springy.

"I don't think the club will ever go back to what it was, which is a shame in some ways because Springfield Park was very homely. Someone recently

Players looking at a model of the new JJB Stadium

The seats begin to go in at the JJB Stadium

gave me a photograph of the ground during a night game. It was just after we took over there. The terraces were sparsely populated and there were weeds growing up between the concrete. The photograph is titled 'Field of dreams'. It touches my heart when I look at that."

Spencer has a similar emotional attachment to the ground.

"I never went back to Springfield Park after we moved to the JJB until *Sky Sports* came up to do something on the club. I went there to film with them and as we drove up I noticed that the streets leading up to the ground were still exactly the same. It was very emotional. When you've seen the club struggle and come through that you can't help but get emotionally tied up with it."

Nick Bitel is less sentimental.

"Whelan has brought in managers and players but the real impetus at Wigan has been the move to the new stadium. It has enthused the fans to start coming back and I don't think that could ever had happened if they'd stayed at Springfield Park."

It wasn't a given that the fans were going to suddenly start flocking to the JJB. Despite selling a record 1,780 season tickets there was a long way to go to fill it.

"The scale of the new stadium was hard to comprehend," says Spencer. "You have to remember that we were only getting average crowds of 1,800 when Dave took over. From 1995-99 he put some money into the club and we built things up and started getting average crowds of 3,000. That was just before we moved to the JJB. But that was a long way short of 25,000 so we had a lot of work to do to fill it."

Not everyone was sad to see Springfield Park redeveloped

New manager John Benson, who had finally been persuaded by the board to take the job after refusing it the season before, was the man charged with building a team to attract the fans to the JJB. And the Latics took to their new ground like ducks to water. The first league match at the stadium was a 3-0 whitewash of Scunthorpe which saw Simon Haworth score the first competitive goal at the stadium. From then on the ground became a fortress as the Latics went on an unprecedented 24 league match unbeaten run to top the Nationwide League Division Two. Incredibly, the team would not be beaten in the league until January 7, 2000 by which time the club was two points clear at the top of the table.

The fans were slowly starting to fill the ground too. 7,481 turned out for the club's first fixture of the season and 10,531 were there to watch the Latics lose to Wolves in the FA Cup third round. That came on the back of a late September exit from the League Cup. It wasn't to be a good season for cup competition at the JJB. The Latics, as defending champions, were also knocked out of the AutoWindscreens Shield early.

After getting off to such a tremendous start in the league the fans, and the chairman alike no doubt, must have felt that automatic promotion seemed certain. Benson had inherited a decent squad but he had added some extra quality that Mathias had said the squad was lacking the previous season. Benson brought in Kevin Nicholls from Charlton for £600,000, Alan McLoughlin from Portsmouth for £260,000, Neil Roberts from Wrexham for £450,000 and Neil Redfearn from Bradford for £112,500.

One other bit of business that Benson did that season was to bring Arjan De Zeeuw in on a free transfer from Barnsley. De Zeeuw would go on to become a permanent fixture at the back for the Latics in his two spells at the club. The Dutchman's first impressions of the club show how it was already trying to do things in Premiership style.

"The chairman sent his private plane for me and then picked me up from the airfield in his helicopter. I think it was an attempt to try and sway me. I was very impressed with the stadium, less so the training ground then, but it was definitely a club that was looking to go places."

Lee McCulloch, who would sign from Motherwell in March 2001, was given the same five star treatment.

"I didn't know anything about Wigan Athletic before I joined. I got picked up by the chairman's helicopter in Scotland and flown down for a tour of the stadium. It was amazing. The whole thing was a great experience and I thought that they must mean business. The chairman said to me, 'Give us three or four years and this club will be in the Premiership'. I thought that was a bit tongue-in-cheek but the whole set up was definitely geared to getting out of the Second Division."

To do so the Latics would be required to maintain their good form in the second half of the season. Benson's team could not sustain their unbeaten run, however. After being beaten for the first time in the league that season on January 7, 2000 by local rivals Oldham Athletic, it would take the Latics nine games to record their next victory. The dip in form caused the club to

John Benson

drop from first to fourth in the table. From looking at automatic promotion just weeks earlier the club was now fighting to stay in the play-off places. With a total season spend of £1,422,500 – a king's ransom in Division Two – it is easy to see why the chairman might have become a little perturbed when form started to deteriorate in the New Year. Based on past history, another failed attempt at promotion that season would surely cast a shadow over Benson's future at the club.

Benson's team bounced back again, however. A 1-0 win against Reading on April 2, 2000 saw them climb back up the table to second. With three games to go they had a two point cushion over third and seemed in pole position to clinch automatic promotion. But it was not to be. The Latics see-saw form saw them pick up just one point from their remaining fixtures – all against mid-table teams with nothing to play for. It was a massive disappointment for a team that was easily good enough to have gone straight up. Yet again Wigan were destined for the lottery that was the Second Division play-offs.

With the Manchester City experience so fresh in their minds neither players nor fans were particularly enthused by the prospect of the play-offs. Fifth place Millwall, who the Latics had drawn twice with that season, were first up in the Division Two play-off semi final. A nil-nil draw at The New Den left everything to play for at the JJB. A win was paramount. People at the club felt that 10,642 fans turning out to watch was a small victory in itself. The club was slowly but surely winning over lapsed football fans in the town.

The match itself was a tense affair and the only thing to separate the sides was a deflected Darren Sheridan strike in the second half. As the ball trickled through the Lions' goalkeeper's legs into the net the JJB Stadium erupted and, after a tense closing period, the Latics could start looking forward to

Arjan de Zeeuw

playing Gillingham in the play-off final at Wembley. Their last memory of the national stadium was an overwhelmingly positive one.

The play-off final against third place Gillingham would be as hard to call as the semi-final. The Latics had won one and lost one to the Gills in the league that season. Ahead of the final, Benson informed his players that he was to resign as manager and move back into the boardroom. If the Latics' players needed any more motivation for winning promotion this was it. Benson's resignation was seen as inevitable in some quarters.

"The fans never took to him like they had Mathias," says former WISH FM sports reporter and current Media Manager, Matt McCann. "Ray had been a cult hero at the club and the fans saw Benson's hand in his sacking. John got sick of the flak toward the end of the season and fell on his sword."

A massive crowd of 53,764 fans crammed into Wembley to watch Gillingham face a Wigan team that had been bookies' favourites for automatic promotion at the start of the season. The Latics dominated the first half and were unlucky not to take the lead when Andy Liddell's 30 yard piledriver crashed off the bar. It was completely against the run of play when the Gills took a 1-0 lead on 36 minutes when Pat McGibbon deflected a Carl Asaba cross into his own net.

The Latics were lucky not to go two down early in the second half but were soon on level terms when Simon Haworth converted a Liddell centre just under an hour into the match. Just moments later the Latics could have sealed victory when Arjan De Zeeuw headed the ball powerfully towards goal. De Zeeuw was convinced he'd scored and later video replays would show that his header had in fact been cleared from behind the line – but the goal was not given. De Zeeuw was stunned. The goal would have had extra significance for him that day.

I would have given anything for him to see me score the winner at Wembley

"It was the last game my dad ever saw me play. He died soon after and I would have given anything for him to see me score the winner at Wembley. That goal would have put us into Division One (later renamed the Championship). I was so desperate to play there and if that goal had counted I never would have left Wigan for Portsmouth. I stayed another year with the Latics but I started to wonder if we would ever win promotion. As I was

Wigan line up for the Play-off Final against Gillingham

getting older time seemed to be running out."

Time was running out for the Latics in the final too. With four minutes to go Kevin Sharp was shown a red card for a second bookable offence. With the game destined for extra time it would be a telling decision. Against the odds the Latics went 2-1 up in the first half of extra time when Stuart Barlow scored his 23rd goal of the season from the penalty spot after Sheridan had been upended in the box. The Latics fought tooth and nail, expending every last ounce of effort and somehow held onto their narrow lead until five minutes from the end of extra time. By then the 15,000 or so Latics' fans who'd made the long journey down were starting to believe that promotion to The Championship was theirs. Justice had been done for the loss to Manchester City the season before it seemed.

Any premature celebrations that had started were brought to an abrupt end when Gillingham substitute Steve Butler fired a header past Latics' keeper Derek Stillie. At 2-2 with minutes remaining it looked like both sides would settle for penalties but the Gills had other ideas. Ty Gooden, who had crossed for Butler's equaliser, swung another cross into the box as the game went deep into injury time. Another Gills sub, Andy Thomson, somehow got to the ball ahead of Stuart Balmer and the ball flew over Stillie's head into the net. The Latics' promotion dreams had been dashed again.

The defeat was a blow to the club. It could so easily have gone up in the 1999/00 season but astonishingly, considering how much money Whelan was pumping into the club for transfer fees and wages, the club would face an agonising wait before they finally got out of the division. They'd return to the play-offs again, though. The fans shuddered at the prospect and started to think that the only way they were ever going to get out of the league was to win the damned thing.

11   A MANAGERIAL HOT-SEAT

The next man into the managerial hot seat at the JJB Stadium would come with a massive reputation. Former Scotland captain Bruce Rioch arrived at Wigan Athletic having won promotions with Middlesborough (twice) and Bolton (where he also led the club to the League Cup final) and having had a successful spell at Arsenal, where he took the club into the UEFA Cup as well as signing Dennis Bergkamp. Rioch was exactly the type of experienced manager that the club needed to bring stability and lead them up the divisions. It is said he pipped Wigan-born Danny Wilson to the post.

Rioch's last job had been at Norwich City but he'd left the East Anglian club after accusing them of having a lack of ambition. The polar opposite was the case at Wigan Athletic. Rioch looked like the perfect man for the job. He recalls how it all came about and shares his first impressions of the club:

"An agent called me up in June 2000 and asked if I'd be interested in meeting to discuss the vacant manager's position at Wigan Athletic. I was, so a meeting was set up with Benson and Whelan. I had a good discussion with them both and then John came to see me in Norwich and offered me the job.

"I thought Whelan was a super guy. He was very positive. He was a man who was extremely determined, who was motivated, who was driven by the desire to be successful. The ambition ran through that club like blood through your veins. The fact that it was coming from the top down was great. He was determined to take the club into the Premiership. There were no grey areas in that respect.

"The atmosphere at the club was great. It was really forward-thinking. There were some areas at the club that needed some work. It needed catering at the training ground and some infrastructure work but it would all get done in due course. The stadium was fantastic but it was clear that they were only going to fill it in the Premiership. It represented a great challenge for me."

Rioch got off to a great start. In his first ten league games that season the Latics won five, drew four and lost just one. They sat fifth in the league and home crowds were regularly in the region of 6,000. Indeed, by Christmas the Latics had only lost three times in all competitions and were sitting fourth in the league, just two points off top spot. The club's December 23, 2000 fixture against Stoke City was watched by 8,957 – a great crowd for the league.

The club was disappointingly knocked out of the FA and League Cups in the second round of each, however. It was a hat-trick of second round cup KOs when Wigan were beaten by Walsall in the second round of the Leyland DAF Vans Trophy (formerly the AutoWindscreens Shield). Still, as the New Year was ushered in, the club sat second in the league, just two points behind old foes Millwall and everything looked rosy.

"We got off to a great start," enthuses Rioch. "We had a good spell from the start of the 2000/01 season right up until Christmas. There were good foundations at the club but there were things that had to be improved. We knew that things couldn't be changed overnight. Some players' contracts took a while to expire, some players took longer to be moved out than expected but we felt we needed to move on and bring in some fresh faces.

"I looked at the players I'd inherited. There were some there who could do a job for us. There were some that we felt needed replacing. We never had an open chequebook though. I'd go to Benson first, then Whelan and tell them who I wanted and generally he would write the cheque. There was a lot of support in that respect."

That was an understatement. Rioch would spend over £2m in his time at the club which overshadowed most of the other clubs in the league put together. The club was quickly gaining a reputation for being the best payers in the league too. It helped to attract players tempted by one last big pay day and who might not otherwise have come. Arguably not the right type of

Bruce Rioch

player for an ambitious club. The policy started to work against the Latics in other ways too. As Ian Halliwell recalls, Wigan's 'Millionaires' title was making them the team that everyone wanted to beat:

"At Peterborough in 2001 I was sitting with some of their injured players and the running joke with them was about what bigshots Wigan were. In his team talk Barry Fry had said to his team, 'This lot are on £4,000 per week, let's get in about them and show these posers what we're all about'. The average wage at Peterborough at the time was £700 per week. Wigan Athletic lost 2-0 that day."

Wigan's 'Millionaires' title made them the team everyone wanted to beat

After a draw and a win against Wrexham and Swansea City in the first week of January, the Latics were still second and had closed the gap on table toppers Millwall to one point. There was every reason to think that it was going to be a happy New Year indeed. As recent events had shown, however, Wigan Athletic is a club which has always had the capacity to spring surprises on their fans. There would be none bigger than when it was announced in late February that Rioch was leaving the club, which was just a point off the automatic promotion spots when the announcement was made. Whether Bruce resigned or was sacked remains a mystery.

"We were near the top of the table when I left," says Rioch. "I had a disagreement with Whelan on a footballing matter. That's all I want to say about it. It doesn't matter if I left or if I was sacked. If you have a disagreement with the owner of the club there's only going to be one outcome – you're going to leave. I wouldn't use the word frustrating about what happened at Wigan. Disappointing would be a better word. We were doing well when I left and were in with a good chance of getting promotion. It was sad – but it happens in football. There are other sides to the beautiful game."

There are differing opinions as to why Rioch left the club.

"Rioch took the club to second in the league but the team was faltering and the goals were drying up," says Matt McCann. "The chairman and some of the staff, for whatever reason, couldn't take to Rioch. Some said, in football parlance, he'd 'lost the dressing room'."

An account of an incident witnessed by former Latics manager Ian McNeill sheds more light on the situation.

"I went back to Wigan for a third time in the summer of 2000 as a scout but I ended up falling out with the club for the way they treated Rioch. After one match there was a ladies table in the hospitality area and Bruce was there with his wife. The chairman went over to the table and had a go at Bruce for something he'd done during the match. Bruce just got up with his wife and walked out. Soon after he got sacked."

A rumour that adds weight to McNeill's story was circulating at the time. It implied that Rioch had been asked to resign because he objected to Whelan's criticisms after the club's draw with Walsall. In any case Rioch's departure seemed to be as much of a shock to people inside the club as those on the outside. Lee McCulloch, who was Rioch's last signing for the club, was left in a daze by the news.

"Rioch signed me and that same night he got the sack. I didn't know what to expect. It made me have a bit of a shaky start. After the club having so many managers in quick succession I didn't know what to think. My head was all over the place."

Colin Greenhall, who was appointed caretaker manager was equally shocked.

"I got a call asking if I would do the job until the end of the season. It was totally out of the blue and I never expected it."

Greenhall would not see out the rest of the season, however. Having been a great servant to the club as a player he didn't take to management quite so well and struggled to win over a squad he'd only just retired from playing alongside. By the end of his six matches in charge the club had dropped down to fifth in the table, perilously close to slipping out of the play-off places altogether.

Greenhall was only ever going to be a stop gap in any case. Whelan's son-in-law and vice-chairman, Duncan Sharpe, had already sounded out golfing partner Steve Bruce about the position and had received a favourable reply before Greenhall was relieved of his duties. Bruce was a popular choice with the players, particularly De Zeeuw.

"I was looking forward to working with Bruce when he came in. As a centre back he was a hero of mine. When he arrived he was organised and disciplined but also a very nice man."

Bruce had agreed to take over managerial duties until the end of the season. There were six games left of the regular season and it was hoped that Bruce would lead the club to the play-offs if not to the automatic promotion that had seemed so likely up until Rioch's departure. Like his predecessors Bruce was not offered a long term contract by Whelan.

McCann recalls that Bruce immediately lifted the team as it went on to win three, lose two and draw one of the club's remaining fixtures to secure a play-off berth.

"Bruce came in for six games and led the Latics into the play-offs. He lifted the team through his sheer presence and charisma. He was a big name that everyone knew."

The Latics' opposition in the play-off semi-final would be Reading. The Latics had only taken a point off the Royals during the league campaign. The first match at the JJB was played in front of a season's best crowd of 12,638 and was a tense affair. Wigan made all the running in the game and had the ball in the net twice – once from a header that was cleared from behind the line and a second which the referee deemed had been cheekily knocked out of the goalkeeper's hands. Neither counted and the game ended nil-nil.

The second leg was an even more eventful affair. Reading went into the match as favourites to progress to Wembley. No-one could tell the Latics that, however, and after an incident packed 26 minutes a Kevin Nicholls free-kick from just outside the box was fired into the bottom corner of the Royals' net. Advantage Wigan. The Latics defended their lead heroically and were lucky

Bruce Rioch with the squad, 2000/1

Steve Bruce

not to concede on a couple of occasions. Reading looked dead and buried as the game entered the 86th minute and Latics' fans had already started to dream of Wembley. They'd been down this road before, however. And not just once. As the clock ran down Reading substitute Nicky Forster broke down the right, went past two Wigan defenders and crossed the ball for a waiting Martin Butler to fire it into the net.

The Latics' players and fans were shellshocked and after a couple of minutes of prolonged celebration the match restarted. Latics' fans eyed the clock nervously because Reading clearly had the momentum. The game settled down briefly and extra time looked a certainty. Until Forster picked up the ball, burst into the box and was dragged down for a penalty that is. Jamie Cureton stepped up to take the spot kick for the Royals. It seemed to take an eternity for him to strike the ball and when he did Roy Carroll leapt to his left to palm the ball away. There was a split second when Latics' fans celebrated wildly but Forster was on hand to knock in the rebound. It was play-off heartbreak for the Latics for the third time. Everyone connected to the club, from fan right up to chairman, was dumbstruck.

No-one blamed Bruce for the defeat and it was expected that he'd stay on for the following season to try for promotion again. It was mooted in the press that he was going to receive a £5m war chest from Whelan to support the cause. As McCann highlights, everything seemed to point toward Bruce staying.

"At the end of the season Bruce released nine players. He was clearing the decks for his new regime. The feeling amongst the fans, with the press, and at the club was that he would be there come the start of the 2001/02 season."

Bruce's axe-wielding didn't make him a popular figure with the fans during the close season, however.

"Bruce is not liked in Wigan," says Halliwell. "The last job Whelan told him to do was to cut out the dead wood from the club. He sold a lot of the club's cult figures who Whelan thought were just there to pick up their wage packets."

But Whelan's seeming reluctance to tie his managers into long term contracts would come back to haunt him. Bruce was not destined to be in charge of the Latics come the start of the following season.

Bruce's axe-wielding didn't make him a popular figure with the fans

"Everyone thought that he was going to get the job permanently," says De Zeeuw. "But then suddenly at the end of May Crystal Palace came in for him."

According to Whelan, there was nothing he or Duncan Sharpe could do to persuade Bruce to stay.

"Steve put his cards firmly on the table and told me that he had thought about it for over a week and it was an offer he couldn't refuse. We didn't even have the chance to offer him a package with Wigan."

It may have been an amicable split but it didn't change the fact that Wigan's chairman had got through a record three managers in one short season. Of equal concern was that they were still in the Second Division. It frustrated everyone. The fans were frustrated by Whelan's incessant tinkering and failure to hold onto a manager. It was frustrating for the players too, because no sooner had they proved themselves under one manager than another came in. Patience in the dressing room was running out and each new manager that came in was having a harder time trying to unite the disparate group of long-serving pros, players that their predecessor might have brought in, and fresh faces they would bring in themselves.

Mathias who had been sacked two years earlier feels that the management merry-go-round was at the root of the club's underachievement.

"My sacking put huge pressure on Benson to come in and get promotion. The managers after John were under the same pressure. I don't think it helped the club chopping and changing managers so often. They'd all bring in their own players and it made it impossible to get a settled side. They were never going to get promoted the way they were going."

Whelan was frustrated too. He'd already spent the better part of £40m on the stadium and the squad and was desperate for the club to get out of the Second Division.

"Missing out on success definitely does get you down," said Whelan in a revealing interview with the *Manchester Evening News* at the time. "Having to get on with life after disappointment is not as easy as it sounds. Our supporters know all about depression — I have never known a club endure as much bad luck as Wigan have in recent times. It's been one tale of disappointment after another — all we can do is wait and see what the new season brings but we are just as determined.

"We all work very hard at Wigan — we want success and surely it's time we got something in return. We are still in what is going to be a very tough Second Division. This time last year a lot of people said promotion was on but it just didn't happen. Losing to Reading in the closing minutes hurt. Like I say it's a very tough division to get out of and you have to be prepared to scrap it out."

Whelan's words give a hint that he'd finally realised that promotion wasn't going to come overnight. That greatest of virtues, patience, was required. Maybe that meant Whelan finding a manager who he was comfortable giving his long term backing as opposed to handing him a week-to-week contract. If a manager could be found who struck the right chord with the chairman, one who he was prepared to back to the hilt, there was no limit to what the club could achieve.

12   HONESTY & GRAFT

With an unruly dressing room, expectant fans, and tens of millions already invested in the club, Whelan's next management hire was key. Despite the managerial musical chairs that had gone on at the club since he had taken over, which had seen seven managers come and go in six years, there was a host of big names interested in the job. John Aldridge, Kenny Dalglish, Roy Evans, Sammy McIlroy, Jan Molby, Ronnie Moore, Bryan Robson and Joe Royle were all linked to the club. Whelan was spoilt for choice but he had two basic criteria for his new charge:

"I simply want honesty and graft, and a manager who rolls his sleeves up and works hard. If someone is prepared to do that, they can be very successful here."

One manager not initially linked with the job but who matched the criteria perfectly was Paul Jewell. Jewell had just left the manager's post at Sheffield Wednesday under a cloud. Having played for Wigan in the 1980s and led Bradford City to the Premiership and kept them up in his first managerial role, he seemed to be an ideal candidate for ambitious Wigan. At 36, he might have been considered too young for the job by some. One person who didn't fancy the former Liverpool player for the position was Harold Ashurst. Ashurst, who had famously penned a piece for the *Wigan Observer* in 1978 writing off the club's chances of getting elected into the Football League, stuck his head on the line again.

"There were a number of top names in the frame for the Wigan job after Bruce went to Palace," says Ashurst. "I said on *WISH FM*, 'Anyone but Jewell'."

Ashurt would soon be made to eat his words as co-presenter Matt McCann recalls:

"Jewell was a late applicant for the job that summer. John Benson went to see Paul and liked what he had to say. He persuaded the chairman that Jewell was the man for the job. The chairman will probably say he was the number one choice but there were others in the frame."

By June 11, 2001, Jewell and his former assistant at Bradford, ex-Chelsea player Chris Hutchings, were installed as the Latics' new management team. Despite the flurry of interest from many more experienced candidates Jewell recalls that the interview process was extremely informal:

"I lost my job at Sheffield Wednesday in February. I was playing a bit of golf and relaxing. It was the first time I'd had any time off work since I was 16. I got a call from someone at the club about the job and went to meet Benson. We had a half hour chat and he offered me the job the next day."

Having played for the Lancashire club for four seasons between 1984 and 1988, during which time he scored 35 times in 137 appearances, Jewell thought he knew the club inside out. He'd discover on his first day in charge that nothing could be further from the truth.

"I thought I knew about Wigan Athletic from my playing days but when I walked through the door I realised that I didn't. It was all changed from when I was here. There was a training ground and a new stadium for starters. I hadn't met Whelan by that time and he came to see me. We shook hands and went out for a long walk across the pitches. He said, 'There's a lot of nonsense spoken about me, about me interfering and this, that and the other. I just want you to get on with things and do your job'."

Whelan's direct approach appealed to Jewell who had signed a two year contract with the club. He was the first manager to be afforded this level of support from Whelan from day one. Hutchings was similarly impressed and relished the challenge ahead.

"I'd just been sacked as manager at Bradford, where I'd worked with Paul when we got promotion to the Premiership. You could tell when you walked in the door at Wigan Athletic that it was geared for success. It was the right time for the club. The chairman was willing to invest in success – not just buy it – the stadium was there and the fans deserved it. We came and got everyone moving in the right direction. The most important thing was to get out of Division Two and then we had a five year plan to get out of that division. But that was our belief, not the chairman's or anyone else's."

Jewell's appointment met with the approval of one former manager.

"Paul is an ex-Wigan player," explains Bruce Rioch. "He would have had a tremendous affinity and feel for the club having played at Springfield Park so I thought it was a good appointment."

Jewell and Hutchings were very much their own men from the start. They knew what was required, communicated it to the chairman and won his trust and support immediately. Fans and players alike had been calling for some time for the chairman to get someone in who would be given time to build a team that could enjoy lasting success. There had been too many

Paul Jewell

quick fixes in the past. Those inside the club saw straight away that Jewell and Whelan were going to get on.

"When Paul came in I think Whelan recognised that this was someone he could get behind and give a bit of time to overhaul the whole club," says Jewell's former club captain Alex Cribley. "Paul and Dave seemed to hit it off straight away. Paul calls a spade a spade and doesn't suffer fools gladly, much like the chairman. I think he was quite frank about what needed doing and the chairman took notice."

The significance of Jewell being the first manager under Whelan to be offered a long term contract was not wasted on Hutchings.

"There hadn't been much stability at the club before we came along," says Hutchings. "There'd been quite a few managers in quick succession and Paul was the first one to sign a proper long-term deal. But the chairman wanted stability as well. It's important to recognise that. It's hard to do anything at a club when the management changes so frequently. It doesn't help the players, the staff, the chairman or the fans. The chairman backed us from day one. That gave us the time to do what we wanted to do. We just needed to start getting the results. That came through really hard work."

In retrospect it was just as well that Jewell had the chairman's support. After a pitiful first month in charge during the 2001/02 season, Jewell's team was sitting fourth from bottom in the Nationwide League Division Two and had again been knocked out of the League Cup early. It was a nightmare start for Jewell, who struggled to get to grips with the unsettled squad of players he'd inherited.

McCann underlines just how unruly the dressing room had become:

"One player who'd been disciplined by Jewell said to him, 'You can fine me what you want. In a few months time you're not going to be here – I will'."

Fine me what you want. In a few months you're not going to be here – I will

And it was about to get worse. The Latics crashed out of the Leyland DAF Vans Trophy on October 16, 2001 after being beaten 5-1 by a Wrexham team that were two places below them in the table. It was crisis point and the season was barely a month old. Jewell would need to hope that the chairman was as good as his word.

"It didn't start well at all," said Jewell painfully, speaking in 2006. "I didn't like a lot of the players. The culture in the dressing room was not good. In fairness to the players that culture might not have been helped by the manager changing so often. There was no stability but I felt that there were players who were not pulling their weight.

"The first season was all about trying to sort it out. I told the chairman that there was an atmosphere at the club that I didn't like. There was no togetherness about the place like we have now. The real low point was losing to Wrexham. After that I went to see the chairman and said, 'I'm really struggling with this squad'. He went straight down to the dressing room. 'He's staying', he said to the players. 'If you don't want to stay, that's fine, but he's here to stay'. He backed me there when I needed it. I think it's easy to back someone when things are going well. I always judge people by how they treat you when your back is against the wall. It would have been an easy choice to change the manager again then."

Whelan was more than happy to back Jewell. Despite his ambition he could see that there were elements holding back progress that were out of the young manager's control.

"Jewell is doing a good job but will need time before his new-look team is the finished article," said Whelan to the *Manchester Evening News* at the time. "Players have come and gone. It's definitely a rebuilding phase. No-one can put an ounce of blame on Jewell for what has gone on so far this season. I admit results have been disappointing but the lad has my full support and I am going to ride the storm alongside him.

"When Paul became manager I told him this was going to be a difficult job. This club was in need of a damned good shake-up from top to bottom. We have some good players but they are being let down by those who have no heart or bottle. To an extent we have had to start from scratch."

Arjan De Zeeuw remembers it as a turning point for the club.

"We had a difficult group of players when Paul came. Some weren't pulling their weight, some had a problem with the manager and there were too many little cliques. It was a very difficult situation for the manager. He did well though. He stuck to what he thought was right. When we had a bad start to the season and we were in the bottom three, a lot of the players were thinking that Paul was going to get the sack. A lot of people were saying, 'You know what the chairman is like...'.

"But the chairman stuck by Paul. He came to the dressing room and stood up for him. 'He's staying,' he said to the players. 'You should take a long hard look at yourselves instead of waiting for him to go.' It was an important moment in the history of this club because it was crying out for some stability. It was important for Paul because a lot of the players weren't interested in playing for him or impressing him because they thought he was going to leave anyway. That sort of thing kills a football club."

Hutchings has similarly vivid memories of the day:

"The chairman did come down to the dressing room and speak to the squad. It made those players who were biding their time until Paul got sacked sit up and take note. When you take over somewhere there's always a period of unrest. The players don't know if you'll want to keep them and it's very difficult to move players on, especially if they are on good contracts. We had to stick with it and come through that."

It was a great show of support from Whelan, especially if you remember that Rioch had been forced out of the club when the Latics were in the top six. The Latics were worse off than ever and Jewell had already spent £1.55m bringing in Peter Kennedy, Jason De Vos and Tony Dinning. But Whelan's vote of confidence did Jewell the world of good and things started to turn around for the club from then on. Jewell wasn't able to just wave a magic wand and make things better, however. He'd won back the dressing room but it would be a gradual process to turn things around on the pitch.

Defender Matt Jackson played his first game for Jewell following the LDV Trophy defeat to Wrexham:

"Ironically, my first game was Wrexham at home in the league the following Saturday," says Jackson. "We lost 3-2 having conceded two goals against ten men. It didn't look like it could get any worse. It was grim. We were second bottom, the manager was under a bit of pressure and it wasn't the best bunch of lads in the dressing room. On the Tuesday night we went to Tranmere and won 1-0 though. From then on we moved up the league. We lost quite a lot but we started picking up more points and moved out of the bottom three."

The Latics sat fourteenth in the league by Christmas but were by no means out of the relegation mire. Following the nadir of Wrexham there was one last disappointment for Jewell in the first half of the 2001/02 season. After losing to non-league Canvey Island in the FA Cup almost a month to the day of the Wrexham defeat, the manager wondered if he'd ever be able to get the club moving in the right direction.

"I met Paul for a drink after the Canvey Island game," says Jewell's close

Paul Jewell & backroom staff 2001/02.
Left to right (top): Stuart Welsh, A.May, Alex Cribley. (bottom) Colin Greenall, Paul Jewell, Chris Hutchings

friend, Graham Barrow. "He wasn't sure if he could turn things around in the short time he had."

The young manager was starting to question whether he'd bitten off more than he could chew.

"I shipped a few players out after the Wrexham game and I brought Jeff Kenna in on loan," says Jewell. "We won straight away against Peterborough but then lost at home to Colchester. Then we beat Stoke City 6-1 but got knocked out of the FA Cup by Canvey Island. That was a low point. It was real stop-start stuff that season as there were certain players in the team who weren't up to it. I didn't find that commitment and desire that my team at Bradford City had. There was no will to win. I found that difficult. I wouldn't say that I considered quitting but you do start to question your own ability

Latic's pre-match warm-up, 2001/2002

when things aren't going well. I just wanted to see out that season somehow and plan for the next."

After the Canvey Island defeat, Hutchings recognised that the pair could ill afford any more slip ups.

"Losing to teams like Canvey Island caused a lot of doom and gloom. We knew that we had to turn it round and put pressure on ourselves to do it even quicker. We knew the chairman was putting a lot of money into the club and he wanted a return. He was entitled to that. We had his backing but in football you know that if things go badly you're out the door."

After Canvey Island things looked up for Jewell. He led the club on an unprecedented (for the season) eleven game unbeaten run in the league to climb to thirteenth in the table by January 19, 2002. It wasn't anywhere near what Whelan had demanded when Jewell had taken the job. However, it was a hell of a lot better than bottom of the league where the Latics had been a couple of months earlier.

At the heart of the good run was Jewell's success in overhauling the squad. With a war chest bolstered by the sale of Roy Carroll to Man Utd for a club record £2.5m, the Liverpudlian embarked on a wholesale personnel change. Jewell brought in John Filan from Blackburn for £600,000, Gary Teale from Ayr for £200,000, Jason Jarrett from Bury for £75,000 and most notably Nathan 'The Duke' Ellington from Bristol Rovers for a club record £1.2m.

Despite the big figures, and fellow Second Division clubs' continued accusations that Wigan Athletic were trying to buy the league, Jewell's net spend for the season was only £990,000. Bruce Rioch points out that far from being extravagant, Jewell's forays into the transfer market were very astute.

"His purchases have been extremely good. They have been wise and they have paid dividends for him and the club."

Rioch is right. Ellington scored goals for fun at the club and Filan, Jackson and Teale would continue to be great servants to the club for many seasons to come. The wisdom of Jewell was that he used Wigan Athletic's ability to pay some of the best salaries in the division to attract players who were actually good enough for the division above. It was that sort of foresight that attracted Matt Jackson, who had Premiership experience, to the JJB.

"Wigan were a bit ahead of the game wages-wise in that division but the manager was buying players for the next division up. That is why they were always going to do so well in getting promotions. It's been about getting players to buy into the potential at the club and seeing that they are not signing for a Second Division team, rather a Championship team in waiting. The real investment was made by the club becoming one of the best payers in the division. They weren't the only club paying good wages then though. There were eight other clubs that could match what Wigan paid, Cardiff being one. But it was a question of the potential."

Despite its spending power, in the Jewell era Wigan Athletic ceased signing players who were content just to pick up their sizable pay packets at the end of every week.

When Jewell first arrived at Wigan he called it the gravy train

"When Jewell first arrived at Wigan he called it the gravy train," says club Media Manager, Matt McCann. "He reckoned players came to Wigan for the last big pay day of their careers and disappeared off the radar. There was only really Roy Carroll during that era who came here and went on to bigger things."

One thing Jewell and Hutchings could never be accused of was wasting money. Jewell's canniness is thought to be another facet of his character that endeared him to Dave Whelan. The young management team operated a discerning transfer policy which persists to this day.

"It's okay having money but you've got to be careful how you spend it," explains Hutchings. "We don't just sign anyone. We go into their background, look at how they play. We work hard and we expect our players to work hard and we don't suffer fools gladly. If we need a player we look at who's available. We'll get together with our scouts and look at all the options and pick our first choice, second choice etc. We'll go over the list with the chairman. He's played the game at the highest level and he knows what the game is all about. If he doesn't like someone it won't stop us buying them. It's just doubly important that they perform. We've always had money to spend but you don't just go out and spend it because it's there. It's not an open chequebook. Paul and I ask ourselves, 'What do we want? Do we need it? And, can we manage without it?' That's the process."

At the same time as recruiting a group of players who would stay at the club over the next three or four seasons and prove almost to a man to be excellent signings, Jewell cut the squad mercilessly. No fewer than thirteen first team squad members moved on during the 2001/02 season and the clearout started having the desired effect.

"As a senior pro I think I understood more about the pressure that Paul and Chris were under," says Matt Jackson. "The work ethic at the club was poor but they brought in myself, Kenna and Filan and alongside existing players like De Zeeuw, McCulloch and McMillan we brought a bit more discipline into the dressing room and led by example. A couple more players came in and things started to look up. We started to move up the league and we got on a bit of a charge and people were talking about us making the play-offs."

McCulloch echoes Jackson's thoughts:

"I had not been playing well because I'd been unsettled by the high turnover of managers. But then Paul came in and my performances started picking up. There were a lot of players in the dressing room then who had a real problem with the number of managers that had been through the door. They were just happy to sit there, not perform and pick up their pay packet. The manager moved them on and brought players in who were hungry and things started improving from there on in."

De Zeeuw is also in accord:

"Over time Paul got the players in that he wanted and turned things around. He was ruthless in a way. He said to the ones that he didn't want at the club that they could go if they found new clubs. There were also some players there who thought they were giving their all but they weren't. The gaffer weeded them out."

The battle for the hearts and minds may have been won but the Latics still had a lot of work to do in the league. Sitting mid-table after its eleven match

Lee McCulloch in full flight

unbeaten run, a play-off berth wasn't out of the question if that run of form could continue. But as Jewell's remodelled side struggled to gel, the Latics would lose three and draw one of their next four games. By February 9, 2002 they had slipped down to sixteenth in the table. However, as the spirit in the dressing room brightened and the quality of football improved, Jewell's team would win seven, draw five and lose just two of their last 14 league games. The Latics would end the year tenth in Division Two, just a handful of points shy of the play-off places.

It had been a rollercoaster year. The football hadn't always been good to watch, in fact sometimes it was downright ugly, but as Jewell shaped his squad, people in the town started taking notice. There had regularly been over 7,000 in the stands at the JJB that season.

In a turbulent campaign it seemed like Jewell had done that most tricky of tasks – win over the fans and the chairman. Yet he'd done it having nowhere near the success that his five predecessors had. Jewell had achieved nothing tangible but he had got everyone, players included, to see that the club was poised to mount a serious assault on promotion the following season.

It had been a rocky season. Never more so than in the dressing room following the Latic's 5-1 drubbing by Wrexham. There Jewell's future at the club hung in the balance until the chairman stood shoulder to shoulder with him in an act of unity that defines the club to this day. The incident has gone down in Wigan Athletic folklore, yet few know what Whelan said to his young manager that day as they walked side by side out of the dressing room. The chairman had not gone completely soft.

I want us to be in the top six otherwise you won't be here

"As we walked out," recalls Jewell with a chill, "Dave said to me, 'I expect us to consolidate this year but by next Christmas I want us to be in the top six otherwise you won't be here'."

With Whelan's words still ringing in his ears Jewell left for a well-earned summer holiday with much to ponder.

13   **PROMOTION IS A MUST**

After the chilling warning that Dave Whelan had given his young manager, Paul Jewell knew the chairman meant business. He'd had his bedding-in period and even someone with the most rudimentary understanding of the game knew that after the amount of the chairman's money Jewell had invested the season before, promotion was a must. Anything less would be a failure. Jewell was happy to acknowledge it.

"The aim was to get promotion, and I told the players just that. We had a better squad than the previous year and I knew we would be up there competing for promotion if we played our best."

Jewell's men got off to a flyer. They won the first four games of the season, scoring nine and conceding just two, to go two points clear of Brentford at the top of the table. It's interesting to note the augmenting crowds in the first two home fixtures of the 2002/03 season of 5,837 and 6,548. Come the end of the season the average crowd at the JJB would be 7,283, well up on the 5,771 average from the season before.

The Latic's form dipped slightly following the bright start. They lost to bottom of the table Port Vale and mid-table Colchester United. It was but a blip after which the club went on a 16 match unbeaten run in league and cup. By November 9, 2002 the club were one point clear of Oldham Athletic at the top of the table.

It was in the midst of this run that news began to filter through that club vice chairman Duncan Sharpe had taken his own life following a private battle against illness and depression. It was devastating news for everyone that knew Sharpe, not least his family and his father-in-law Whelan who worked closely with the 43-year-old JJB Sports chairman.

"I miss Duncan terribly. He was a good son and a friend," says Whelan. "Duncan was Wigan through and through. He was a football man – he had a good knowledge of the game and most importantly youth was on his side. He was also a good supporter of Paul Jewell. I wanted Duncan to take charge of the club – the time was right."

Sharpe's death hit the Latics fans hard too. It is said that when Whelan was wavering on whether to buy the club in 1995 it was Sharpe who talked him round. He was seen as Whelan's heir apparent at Wigan Athletic and his death

Paul Jewell wins the Manager of the Month Award, December 2002

had robbed the club of a natural successor to Whelan.

Only in the fullness of time will Latics fans truly learn what the sad loss of the devoted husband and father of four will mean for the club. There are many Latics fans in the Whelan clan, including Sharpe's two teenage sons. But for many, Sharpe was one in a million: an astute businessman, a thoroughly decent man and a Latic to the very core. Whichever way you looked at it the club had lost someone on whom it relied for its continued survival. At the most basic level it had lost one of its biggest fans.

With the team seriously in the hunt for automatic promotion, the campaign became an ongoing tribute to the memory of its late vice-chairman. Come season-end there was not one player, staff member or indeed fan who would not spare a thought for the memory of the charismatic Sharpe.

With such decent league form you couldn't help get the impression that the LDV Trophy took a back seat during the 2002/03 season. It was no surprise to see the Latics crash out of the tournament in the second round at the hands of Doncaster in front of a measly home crowd of 2,030. The FA Cup provided little joy for the Latics either. The club lost to Stoke in the third round.

The League Cup would be a different story. In the past Wigan Athletic could never claim to have set the competition alight, yet under Jewell the Latics were like a different club. After knocking out Northampton in the first round Wigan were rewarded with a home tie against Premiership side West Brom. In the midst of its confidence-building 16 match unbeaten run the Latics were not fazed by their superior opposition. And it was club record signing Nathan Ellington's hat-trick that sent the Midlands club packing.

The Latics line-up of Filan, Eaden, McMillan, De Vos, Jackson, Teale, Jarrett, Dinning, McCulloch, Roberts, Ellington, eight of whom had been signed by Jewell, was rewarded with a third round home tie with another Premiership side, Manchester City. Andy Liddell was also a key member of the squad though he missed some of the club's biggest matches that season through injury.

With the earlier contentious play-off defeat at the hands of the Blues still fresh in the memories of Latics fans you can only imagine the atmosphere created by the massive 15,007-strong crowd inside the JJB. In probably the best atmosphere inside the stadium to date, a first half Neil Roberts goal for the Latics was the difference between the two teams. The final whistle was greeted with pandemonium.

This was seriously uncharted territory for the club

By this stage in the Latics record-breaking cup run the press were starting to sit up and take notice of the revolution which was gathering pace at the JJB. The Latics were guaranteed more publicity when they drew another Premiership side in Fulham in the fourth round. This was seriously uncharted territory for the club but Jewell's well-drilled unit got off to a dream start courtesy of two goals from Ellington in an eight minute first half spell. Fulham grabbed a late consolation but the Latics marched on to a quarter final match up with yet another Premiership opponent.

In mid-December a record 16,922 crowd turned out to watch the Latics play Dave Whelan's former club and League Cup holders Blackburn Rovers. It was a taste of things to come for the Latics if they could maintain the considerable progress in the league under Jewell. It was a bridge too far to claim a fourth consecutive Premiership scalp, however. A talented Blackburn side boasting the likes of Friedel, Tugay, Yorke and Cole eased to victory over the home side with a double strike by the latter. The loss denied the Latics a fairytale semi-final clash with Manchester United.

In the league, meanwhile, the Latics were putting together another unbeaten run. No sooner had their 16 match league and cup unbeaten run ground to a halt in early November than a league run started which saw the Latics win ten in a row. Incredibly, they did not concede one goal in the league in November or December. By January 18 they were eleven points clear at the top of Nationwide Division Two. It is worth noting that Jewell's team had far surpassed Whelan's target of being in the top six by Christmas. The Latics had already gone four points clear by December 25, 2002.

It must have brought some relief to Jewell to begin to pay back the patience and loyalty shown him by Whelan. Jewell in turn owed a debt of gratitude to his new signings who were to a man proving to be shrewd acquisitions.

"I lost De Zeeuw to Portsmouth at the end of the 2001/02 season which was a blow," says Jewell. "But the next season was the first full one for Jackson, De Vos, Filan and Teale and we got off to a flyer and just never looked back. Ellington, who'd signed in March 2002, was also a major catalyst for that."

It had been a wrench for De Zeeuw to leave in the close season but the guarantee of higher level football proved too tempting.

"I was playing well and I felt like I needed to get out of that division. I knew I had to challenge myself at a higher level. I would have loved to do it with Wigan but the club had only just got some stability and it didn't look like it was going to happen soon. It was difficult to leave the fans. They'd even organised an special day for me when they all wore orange because I'm Dutch. It was 'De Zeeuw day'. Things like that were special and made it very hard to leave. I thought they were going to kill me when they found out I was leaving."

Some fans may well have were it not for the blossoming of the defensive partnership of De Vos and Jackson at the back that season. This eased the pain of De Zeeuw's loss considerably and set the Latics on the road to success.

"There was a bit of pressure on in Paul's second season in charge because of how we'd finished the season before," recalls Jackson. "We lost Arjan which was a bit of a blow but myself and Jason formed a partnership at the back and we got off to a flyer. There was expectation but there was never horrendous pressure because we'd got off to such a good start."

Jackson was right. The Latics good run had given them a comfortable cushion at the top. The penultimate game of their ten match unbeaten streak in the league was the nearest thing that they had to a league decider all season.

"We had a Friday night game in early January," says Jackson. "It was televised on Sky because we were playing Bristol City who were one of our closest rivals for the title. That was probably the hardest game we had all season but we came through it winning 1-0. That put us 12 points clear of them. Once we'd won that we never really looked back."

Following their gutsy away win against Bristol City, the Latics homed in on a first Division Two title. What was significant about Jewell's squad was that he'd only made a couple of modest additions in the current season. The open heart surgery on the team the season before had started to pay off. Players like Jackson, Ellington, Dinning and Filan were combining well with players who had survived the Jewell cull, like McCulloch and Liddell, to form a skilful, competitive squad. Indeed, Jewell's only outlay that whole season was to bring in a promising young midfielder from Peterborough for £275,000. Jimmy Bullard would prove to be one of the best buys in the club's history.

Wigan Athletic's charge to the 2002/03 Division Two title had looked in good shape by Christmas and by March 22 eleven games without defeat had left the Latics twelve points clear at the top. It was a seemingly unassailable lead. However, it would take until April 19, 2003 when Swindon Town beat second placed Crewe to extinguish their hopes that the title and automatic promotion to The Championship would be Wigan's.

The Latics drew 0-0 away to Huddersfield that night but never will such a dull, workmanlike performance be greeted with such hysteria. Scenes of jubilation on the terraces spilled over onto the pitch as Jewell's squad celebrated with their loyal supporters. It was a special moment for a club that had suffered so much bad luck in its history. After 25 years in the Football League they were heading for The Championship (formerly the First Division) for the first time. That quarter century had been peppered with so few highlights. There were just a couple of promotions, a couple of pieces of silverware but an awful lot of suffering.

Latics fans celebrated that night as if they'd won the Champions League. Proving what a tight-knit club it still was, despite the widescale changes, many of the players joined the fans back at their favourite – and indeed only – hangout in the rugby-dominated town, Rik's Bar. Rik's deserves a mention

Paul Jewell holds the Division Two Winners Trophy, 2003

because it was at the epicentre of celebrations as the Latics dominated Division Two that season. The success of Rik's, which would see as many as 1,000 Latics fans through its doors after any given home match, was symptomatic of how attitudes in the town had changed toward the club. It would have been unheard of to have such a bustling bar dedicated to the Latics even five years earlier.

Paul Jewell had maintained a dignified silence in the weeks before the Latics had clinched promotion. Once it had been secured he was full of praise for his team who had surpassed his target of 92 points that season. The club would end the season with a flurry to reach a record 100 points. It is still a source of pride to Jewell:

"The championship was well deserved. We did extremely well away from home which was a major factor in taking us up. The feeling of achievement was just great. We were the best team in the league and I was delighted for everyone associated with the club – it was a special moment that had been waiting to happen."

Hutchings put the club's success down to teamwork:

"It was a big effort on everyone's part. It was good to be working with such an excellent bunch of professionals. Their attitude was there for all to see."

Harold Ashurst, who had famously warned Wigan against hiring Jewell, was glad to be proven wrong.

"Jewell did an absolutely incredible job. Unbelievable. The players would have run through a brick wall for him."

Matt McCann shares those sentiments and is quick to play down the importance of Whelan's wealth in the promotion.

"Paul did not buy his way out of that league. He did it by good management and I say that from an informed, independent position after watching them all season for *WISH FM*."

One man who was not present at Huddersfield to join the fans and players in wild celebrations was Whelan. It was a rare missed game for the chairman but he was as happy as the most ardent Latics fan.

"I'm so proud of what Wigan Athletic have achieved this season," said Whelan. "We have been the best team and everyone would agree with that. The lads have worked so hard. These are wonderful times for the club, and in football such moments are rare. You have to enjoy the moments when they come along and that's what I've been trying to do. I've employed a few managers in my time as everyone knows. Some of them didn't work hard, some did. The ones who do usually get their just rewards. Paul has got his."

A further reward for Jewell was a new two year contract on improved terms. Whelan didn't have to think twice about making the offer. It had taken eight years but the club had finally won its second promotion after six attempts and was one step closer to realising Whelan's Premiership dream. Much had been made in the past about the chairman's lack of patience with managers in a relentless pursuit of glory but with Jewell it had been different. Jewell had been backed when it looked like he was on thin ice. Whelan had given him *carte blanche* on the squad and stood back, perhaps against his instincts, to give the Liverpudlian the chance to turn the club's fortunes round. It was seen as pivotal in steadying and resetting the course of a previously rudderless ship.

> *A further reward for Jewell was a new two year contract on improved terms*

"You've got to give credit to the chairman for the stability he finally brought to the club," says Matt Jackson. "He had a bit of a reputation in the press before Jewell came in, but he gave him all the backing he needed and we never looked back."

Hutchings gives us a unique insight into why he believes he and Jewell received such unilateral support from Whelan:

"Early on in our time here we had some big set-backs, real low points. The chairman was obviously looking at the results which are the bottom line in this job. And you're not given a lot of time to start getting those results. But he could see that we were doing the right things on the training ground and that we weren't wasting money, and more importantly that we were getting the right players in."

When speaking of the success of Wigan Athletic much is made about a perceived shift in how Whelan handled his club manager from 2001 onwards. Some say he learnt patience and he is rightly praised for giving Jewell the time to prove he was the man to turn the club's fortunes around. His backing of Jewell heralded a new dawn at the club. But it is a discredit to Jewell to place all the onus on Whelan for the club's renaissance. It is the attributes that Jewell boasts as a man and a manager, as much as Whelan's apparent mellowing, that would see him enjoy more autonomy than any other manager in the Whelan era.

His backing of Jewell heralded a new dawn at the club

Jewell may have been a young manager but the experience of his previous two jobs had a massive effect on the relationship he'd form with Whelan. There was no more important relationship in the club.

"I had two successful years at Bradford, taking them to the Premiership the first season and staying up the next," said Jewell. "But I left because my relationship with the chairman was becoming untenable. I went to Sheffield Wednesday and knew immediately that it was probably a wrong decision to go there, but I'm glad I went. I was eventually sacked but you learn more about yourself in times of adversity. After that I took time to analyse my role as a manager and what I wanted to achieve. The break did me the power of good.

"My relationship with Dave Whelan has been influenced by my previous experiences. I think I've earned my stripes and don't feel like I have to justify every decision I make to the chairman. When I'm picking the team I don't worry about what he thinks about my selection. I fully respect Dave but I don't stop to consider whether he will agree with what I'm doing. If I think it's the right decision for this football club I'll do it.

"When you first come to the job you do need help and chairmen can lean on you a little and try to influence you. But sometimes their actions are influenced by your own lack of confidence. Dave has never done that to me here. Because of the success I've had he knows I can do the job. He lets me run the football side and, over a period of time, if the results don't come I know the consequences."

Jewell's unique insight into the complex relationship between manager and chairman makes fascinating reading. His confidence, talent and intelligence are what makes him one of the hottest properties in English football and a potential future national coach.

Many have said that Jewell and Whelan are cut from the same cloth. Maybe it was what was missing between Whelan and his previous managers. Maybe they just weren't right for the club. Who knows. But when Jewell came along something clicked. He was a straight talker, a strong personality and a progressive thinker who knew he was destined for success. He had huge potential and Whelan spotted in the blink of an eye that, given the right blend of support and freedom, Jewell could take the club to the very top.

"We have a fine manager in Paul Jewell," said Whelan. "This fellow is a real worker, who relishes a challenge and knows how to graft. We have a very good working relationship. We speak for an hour every week and discuss various football matters. I don't interfere. I leave him alone, and Paul just gets on with the business. It has worked well."

It is clear there is a massive amount of mutual personal and professional respect between Jewell and Whelan. We must not get carried away on the subject, however. Matt McCann's recollection of a conversation he had with Whelan at a barbeque hosted by the chairman to celebrate promotion, serves as a reminder of how the delicate balance of power that exists at the club could be tipped at any given moment.

"Whelan took me to one side at the party and said, 'Never forget Matt, Paul is king and I let him be king'."

14   **A NEW CHALLENGE**

Wigan Athletic in the Nationwide League Division One. It had a good ring to it and Latics fans had to pinch themselves to check they weren't dreaming and really were looking forward to their first season in the second tier of the Football League. It was a long way from the Cheshire League. It had been a great achievement for the club to climb up from the Third Division to the First in six years. It would be an even greater achievement for the club to stay in the league that first season. They were bookies' favourites to come straight back down. It was fair comment. The league was rife with teams of Premiership pedigree.

It was eight and a half years since Dave Whelan had taken over the club. Now it stood at what the ambitious chairman liked tellingly to call the 'gateway to the Premiership'. There was a lot of work to make true the bodacious claim Whelan had made upon buying the club that they'd be playing in the Premiership within ten years. That would mean Jewell's team winning promotion in their first year in the First Division. No-one expected that, not least the young manager. He and Hutchings had said to themselves when they took over at Wigan that once they got the club out of the Second Division it would take no less than five years to get into the top flight.

Jewell wasn't in as much of a hurry as Whelan and resisted spending more of the chairman's money than he had to in the close season. Indeed, before Christmas only goalkeeper Gary Walsh (free transfer) and striker Geoff Horsfield (£1m) came in, the latter to provide some added firepower. Horsfield would only stay a few months at the club and left to join West Brom for the same fee in late December to be replaced by new club record signing Jason Roberts who travelled in the opposite direction for £1.4m. Roberts and Nathan Ellington would go on to form one of the most potent strike forces in the league. Their goals would fire the club to unimaginable heights. It would spell the end for Andy Liddell at the club. The Latics talisman would leave come the end of the 2003/04 season having scored a club record 70 league goals in six years to secure cult status with the fans.

Jewell was sanguine about the lack of pre-season transfer activity:

"I intend strengthening the squad," he told the *Manchester Evening News*. "But I will only bring players in who I know will improve the team. We want

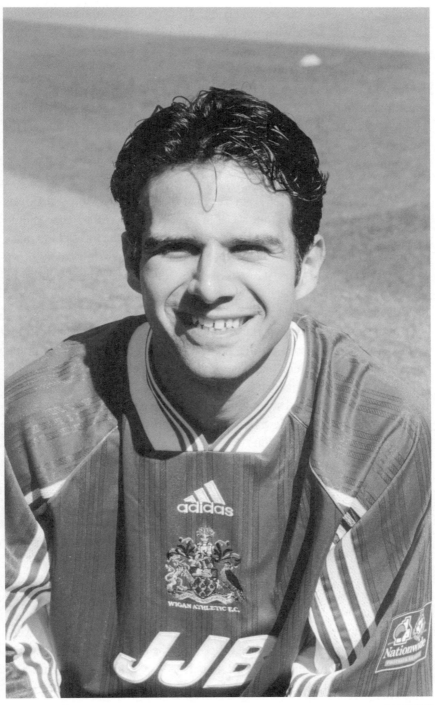

Andy Liddell

to build on last season but we can't go throwing money around and spending for the sake of it. Look what went on at my old club, Bradford. They paid Carbone (Benito) £40,000-a-week and the fans were thrilled at the time, but it bankrupted the club. This is where you have to be sensible."

Jewell's commonsense approach sounded good in theory but, with the squad bereft of new faces, his signing policy of seasons past, namely signing players too good for the league the club were in, would be put to the test for the first time.

Chief scout David Hamilton was sure Jewell's strategy would stand up to scrutiny.

"When I first watched the team they had the likes of Jackson and De Vos playing. I couldn't believe they were in the Second Division. They should have been playing in the league above at least. Paul had the foresight to make the right signings and everyone we took in played their part. It comes down to the fact that Paul is very shrewd. He likes a good deal. There's got to be value for money. Paul doesn't feel like he's spending the club's money, he feels like he is spending his own."

Optimism may have been rife among Latics' fans, a fact reflected in the record season ticket sales during pre-season, but outside of Wigan hopes were not high for the club. That did nothing to dampen the excitement as the club looked forward to its first league match of the season away against old foes Millwall. The fixture list couldn't have thrown up a trickier debut for the Latics than away at The New Den. And so it proved as Jewell's men were defeated 2-0 on August 9, 2003. Welcome to Division One. It was a rude awakening for a team that had walked the league below just months earlier.

"We knew it was going to be tough because we were stepping up a league," says Lee McCulloch. "But losing to Millwall on the opening day of the season was down to lack of belief from everybody in the squad."

Matt Jackson, one of the few Latics players to have previously played in both the Premiership and First Division thought the result may have been a taste of things to come for the club.

"After the first game against Millwall it looked like we were going to be way out of our depth."

Not for the first time that season the Latics would prove that they were made of sterner stuff. They bounced back from the defeat to go on a 16 game unbeaten run, including seven back-to-back wins, in league and cup. The league run left the Latics two points clear of West Brom at the top of the table.

By October 21, the club had beaten Hull City and Premiership Fulham in the first and second rounds of the League Cup too. But Jewell wasn't letting his team take anything for granted.

"I prefer to do things quietly," said Jewell. "All we can do is put things at the back of our minds and get on with what we have to do. As I've said many times before everyone here has their feet firmly on the floor. I'm confident we can handle the extra pressure. I have been in this game a long time and it's what we have done after 46 games that counts."

Jewell's word of caution proved to be timely. The Latics would win again just once during the next eight weeks in which time they lost five, including a 2-1 defeat to Middlesborough in the League Cup. The drop in form caused them to slip to sixth in the table by December 6. Again, Jewell kept his cool:

"There was no doom and gloom. We hit a bad patch but that happens to the best of them."

A December 20, 3-2 victory over Crewe saw the Latics climb back up to fourth in the table but a Boxing Day loss at home to Rotherham in front of 9,235 fans saw the club drop to occupy the last play-off berth. It wasn't disastrous but it wasn't top of the table either and Jewell refused to push the panic button.

It was long-time fan Gorbachev's first game at the JJB

If you happened to drive through Wigan town centre that or any other Boxing Day you would be forgiven for thinking you'd chanced upon a parallel universe. Adhering to a local tradition, the majority of fans wore fancy dress for the festive fixture. Much to the astonishment of the visiting Rotherham fans, the home side were supported by Superman, Batman, Wonder Woman, Julius Caesar, seven Elvises and of-course the Latics most famous fan of all, Mikhail Gorbachev. It was long-time fan Gorbachev's first game at the JJB.

One thing that the club could not disguise was its progress under Jewell. Other clubs were starting to sit up and take notice and, by Christmas, Jewell had already been linked to a couple of 'bigger' clubs. Jewell had no interest in leaving the Latics before he'd completed the job he'd moved there to do. It was Jewell's turn to reciprocate the loyalty Whelan had shown him.

A quick look at the backroom team that Jewell was assembling proved that

Club physio, Alex Cribley

he was there for the long haul. Joining Jewell's former team-mate from the 1986 Freight Rover Trophy final, Alex Cribley, on staff was fellow trophy winner Dave Lowe (youth coach) and David Hamilton (chief scout), who had played alongside Jewell in the 1987/88 season. Jewell's trusted lieutenants knew the club inside out. They were part of its fabric. They had seen success at the club against the odds in the 1980s but had also seen it come within a whisker of going out of existence. They knew what the recent success meant to the fans and Jewell knew he could trust them with his life.

It's such relationships that makes the club special. There's almost a family atmosphere there. From Brenda Spencer, who's spent over 20 years at the club, through to the match day stewards, many of whom made up the 1,500 fans who saw the club through the worst of times, staff at the club know and trust each other and acknowledge the responsibility they have for ensuring that the good times are here to stay.

"There's a good atmosphere at the club," explains Cribley. "All the players and the staff get on well. That's important if you're asking everyone to work their socks off in whatever they do just to keep us in the division. That camaraderie is important. The club has always had that though. Even when I first joined 25 years ago, when we had nothing, there was a good club spirit."

It's a sentiment that David Hamilton echoes:

"Having lots of ex-players on the staff makes a real difference. There's no doubt about that. They have an emotional connection to the club and care what happens to it, which is invaluable."

Jewell also tries to instil this same feeling of affinity in the current crop of Latics players.

"I want to get players here who are loyal, who enjoy their job, who care for their teammates and also care for the club. If you get good players who can do all of that it is a recipe for success."

Matt Jackson confirms that Jewell was succeeding in no small measure.

"Because we know where we've come from and over such a short period of time it serves as a motivation to everyone. The club has grown up together and it is very close in that respect. There are no cliques. All the players and coaching staff know the ground staff and all the staff at the stadium. There is no point in the club being a flash in the pan and that is something that is drilled into you. It is instilled in everyone that comes here that we're building something lasting."

Jewell's relationship with assistant manager Chris Hutchings was also key to the rebirth and continued success of Wigan Athletic.

"They are a team in the truest sense of the word," says Matt McCann. "The gaffer won't sign a new contract until he knows Chris is happy and has signed his."

It will come as a surprise to some to learn that Graham Barrow was almost added to the list of former players in Jewell's backroom staff in the 2003 season. The Chester assistant manager reveals here for the first time how close he came to returning to the club:

"This was never made public but after he'd been there for a couple of seasons Paul sounded me out about going back to Wigan. I told him to check with the chairman first. He did and he didn't say it couldn't happen but I told Paul that I wouldn't do it unless he felt 100 per cent comfortable with it. I could see he wasn't so it never happened."

Being sixth place by Christmas 2003 in their first year in the division was a great achievement for Jewell's team. It was only the half way point, however, and there was a lot of football left to be played that season. A January 3 FA Cup third round showdown with one of the Latics main league rivals would be a good opportunity for the club to prove its credentials for a play-off place. West Ham, who were one point and one place below the Latics in the league, ominously beat the home side 2-1 in a game the Latics should have won, however.

With the Latics out of all cup competitions they could now concentrate on securing a play-off place, if not more. The January 13 signing of Jason Roberts gave the club a much-needed boost – he scored 35 seconds into his debut in a 4-2 away win over Preston – and the club would remain unbeaten in the league during the month to maintain their sixth place spot. They couldn't shake off West Ham who were just two points behind them, however.

In February the Latics won three and drew one to climb up into the top three for the first time in 2004. The run included a 3-1 away win at fifth placed Ipswich Town. The promotion six-pointer was watched by former manager Bruce Rioch.

"Wigan blitzed Ipswich that day," says Rioch. "I thought they were stunning. They were the best team in that division by a mile. Roberts and Ellington looked dangerous. Jimmy Bullard was fantastic in midfield. They ran riot. They had the look of a team destined for promotion."

March was less impressive for Jewell's side. Just when they needed a steady run of form they faltered, losing and drawing twice and registering a solitary victory. Promotion-chasing West Brom were one of the teams to beat the Latics. Their March 16 victory all but secured automatic promotion for them and first placed Norwich. Wigan, sitting seventh, clung onto a vain hope of the play-offs.

In April the Latics indifferent form continued and a nervy nil-nil draw with third placed Sunderland saw the Latics occupy the last play-off spot with two to play. Sixth placed Wigan, fifth placed West Ham and seventh placed Crystal Palace all had 70 points. It could not have been tighter. Third placed Sunderland had just two points more than the trio, while ninth placed Reading were just three points adrift of the play-off places.

The Latics penultimate game in the 2003/04 season was an away fixture against fifteenth placed Nottingham Forest. The disappointing 1-0 loss saw the Latics slip down the table to seventh. A win for West Ham saw then climb up to third, just three points ahead of the Latics. It was all to play for on the final game of the season.

On May 9 a season's best 20,669 fans squeezed into the JJB to watch the Latics go head-to-head with West Ham with a play off place and a potential Premiership place up for grabs. After being top at stages before Christmas some fans were disappointed not to have clinched automatic promotion. But even making the play offs would be a tremendous achievement.

The Latics got off to the best start possible when Neil Roberts fired home a volley to lift the roof at the JJB. The Latics had one foot in the play-offs. Wigan went close twice more early in the second half and Filan heroically denied the Hammers' Bobby Zamora when it looked likely the striker would level the score. With the match in injury time tentative celebrations broke out amongst pockets of the crowd. Mostly amongst those too young to remember the Latics' last minute heartaches in recent seasons. It really looked like the club had done enough this time when Michael Carrick put down the ball to take a free kick with just seconds remaining. It wasn't to be for the Latics, however. Carrick's cross was met by substitute Brian Deane whose equaliser condemned the Latics to seventh place in the league.

It was agonising for everyone associated with the club. The fans had kicked every ball with their team that season. The players had given their all in their first year in the higher division but statistics couldn't lie. Three wins from their last ten games just didn't merit a place in the lucrative Premiership play-offs. McCulloch somehow manages to put a positive spin on the event.

"It was gutting because we conceded a goal in the 92nd minute after looking like we'd done enough to win but we did really well considering we were favourites to go straight back down that year."

Jackson also drew some positives from the experience. It was a sign of how the squad had matured under Jewell.

"It was a major disappointment to miss out on the play offs having been in the top six all season. We knew that we'd have to push on and do better the next season to prove that we could cut it at that level."

Jewell was as disappointed as anyone. He knew his team could have done better, but he was as philosophical as ever in the face of adversity.

"To lose so late was a real kick in the teeth," says Jewell. "I felt empty inside. We were so close and I felt for all the players. It was not a bad effort considering we were labelled relegation certainties at the start of the season. We knew we had to be stronger next time."

There's no hiding that it was a massive disappointment for the club. It was far from a setback, however. Seventh place in what was one of the most closely contested dogfights for

> *To lose so late was a real kick in the teeth. I felt empty inside*

the play-offs in First Division history was a creditable achievement for a team so new to the league. It went a long way toward consolidating the Latics in the division and preparing them for their next campaign.

The entertainment the team had provided in the promotion chase was seeing the club reap the benefits off the field too. The average attendance for the 2003/04 season was 9,530 – over 2,000 more than the previous year. Whelan's foresight had been spot on. If you build it they will come...

Progress was on track off the field but on it Dave Whelan's dream of seeing Premiership football at the JJB within ten years of him buying the club had been dashed. In truth, Whelan was probably the only man in Wigan to believe that it had even been a remote possibility. Still, with a tenacious squad and manager whose zeal matched his own, you couldn't rule out the possibility that the club would win promotion into the top flight in the chairman's tenth year at the helm. Even if it took another ten years it would be an incredible turnaround for a club that had been rock bottom of the Football League with no points and on the verge of financial ruin just a decade earlier.

15   TOP OF THE TABLE

Emboldened by coming so close to reaching the play-offs the season before, the Latics came flying out of the traps for the 2004/05 season. From the opening day of the newly christened Coca Cola Championship season they went on a 17 match unbeaten run hitting top spot on August 15 after beating failed 2003/04 play-off contenders, West Ham, 3-1 at Upton Park. The feat earned Jewell a Manager of the Month award.

By November the Latics had been almost a permanent fixture at the top of the table. There was already a feeling that this could be the Latics' year. Indeed, from the time they first hit top spot, the club wouldn't drop below third place for the entire season. Whether they'd occupy one of the two automatic promotion spots come the end of the campaign remained to be seen.

McCulloch recalls how the hurt of failing to reach the play-offs the season before was used to motivate the squad.

"Everybody remembered the feeling of missing out the season before," says the Scot. "It helped drive our desire and focus for the season ahead."

What is significant and impressive about the Latics performance in the league was that Jewell had again resisted going on a big shopping spree. The club's transfer activity was minimal. Seasoned campaigners De Vos and Liddell left the club and Jewell's main signings were David Wright for an estimated £500,000 and Graham Kavanagh who arrived toward the end of the season for £400,000. 'Kav' was to become a key member of the squad.

It must have taken monumental restraint to not wade into the transfer market after Jewell's squad had run out of steam at the end of the season before. However, the Latics manager was confident that they were coming of age and were more than good enough to win promotion to the top flight. He was tiring of accusations that the club was still trying to buy success.

"I'm becoming fed-up of people going on about this club's resources and how much money we have spent," Jewell told the *Manchester Evening News* at the time. "I say, just look at what we've spent this summer compared to other clubs – our wage bill won't even be half of what some clubs are paying players in this division. Wage bills don't win you promotion – it's about getting the right blend of players and getting them to play a certain way."

Jimmy Bullard & Jason De Vos , 2003/04

Players like McCulloch had every faith that his manager knew what he was doing. He'd soon have his first international cap to prove it.

"The gaffer's signings were brilliant. Everyone he's brought in has had something to contribute. Many have improved as players too. I hadn't been capped for Scotland when I came here but being at Wigan and playing under Paul has been integral to my getting into the national squad."

Plymouth brought the Latics 17 game unbeaten run to an end on November 6. They were beaten again the following week by QPR and in the last seven games of 2004 the club drew twice, won twice and lost three times. By Christmas the Latics clung onto third spot in the league behind Ipswich and Sunderland and were just ahead of the pack of Reading, Sheffield United, Millwall and West Ham.

The New Year started brighter for the Latics who won three times on the trot without conceding a goal. By January 15 they were looking solid in second spot, two points behind Ipswich and a crucial six points ahead of the chasing group. The club had crashed out of the FA Cup at the hands of Grimsby Town in the first round by this time and had long been out of the League Cup. It didn't concern the fans or manager. The league was the focus.

All the work on the pitch by Jewell's team was being matched off it by the coaching, medical and administrative staff. Every effort was being made by the club to bring its training facilities to a level a potential Premiership side might expect. The improvements that had been made since Whelan bought the club were already starting to pay dividends on the pitch.

Alex Cribley has witnessed all manner of changes in his time with the club:

"Since Whelan got involved there's been a gradual influx of money. It's a massive change from the old days. The physio area used to be in a portakabin and now we've got a dedicated area with a gym and new equipment."

No-one was more aware of the massive changes than the players, however.

"The transformation at the club was incredible," says Matt Jackson. "On the terraces, on the pitch, on the training ground, behind the scenes, everything was coming on in leaps and bounds. There were better people coming to work with us, better players coming in and the opposition was better. Momentum was gathering. We even started getting food at the training ground!"

During pre-season training in June 2006, ahead of his final season in charge of the Latics, Jewell said:

"We're working hard here to improve the club all the time because standing still is tantamount to going backwards."

A work in progress too was the Latics push for automatic promotion in early 2005. In February with the all-important end of season run-in beckoning, the Latics won three and lost two of its five games. As the other occupants of the top of table triumvirate – Ipswich and Sunderland – faltered, the Latics hit top spot on goal difference. The top three couldn't have been closer. They all had 66 points and were set for a league run which would see the Latics meet both teams along the way. The club's destiny was in its own hands and Jewell knew it.

"This is our big chance," Jewell told the *Manchester Evening News*. "We could not be in a better position. I don't want us to look back when we're old and think what might have been. We have to go for it and we will."

Midfielder Jimmy Bullard who was an integral part of the promotion chasing squad reckoned the club was ready to move up to the next level.

"There is real hunger in the dressing room and we are stronger this time round," said Bullard at the time "We'll plug for one another and we know every game from here on in is a cup final. We don't intend to slip up."

Bullard's faith in his teammates would be put to the test in the very next match, a March 5 encounter at the JJB with third placed Ipswich. A staggering 16,744 turned out to watch the two teams fight it out for the valuable three points that could be the difference between entertaining Chelsea in the first match of the following season or Burnley. There was no contest.

Jewell's team threatened to run riot over Joe Royle's Ipswich before eventually running out just 1-0 winners following a controversial penalty. The victory saw Wigan Athletic hold onto top spot in the league but two further wins and a draw in March were not enough to stop Sunderland's return to the top. They were two points clear of the Latics, who themselves were three clear of Ipswich. Jewell was still confident his team had what it took to clinch automatic promotion.

"This time last season the players got a bit nervous because it was the first time a lot of them had played at this level and been in such a position," Jewell told the *Manchester Evening News*. "Hopefully we will be better this time because of that experience and I want them to remain focused. The two teams who keep their nerve will go up and we aren't worrying about anyone else."

That wasn't completely true. The Latics had the small matter of its final seven opponents in the 2004/05 Coca Cola Championship campaign to worry about. The string of matches would see them play four of the seven teams fighting it out for a play-off place, two teams battling relegation and last but by no means least their rivals for automatic promotion, Sunderland. West Ham were up first. Sitting in eighth position and with a play-off place firmly in their sights, the Hammers looked the sharper of the two teams and despite the Latics taking an early lead through Jason Roberts, the London side bounced back to defeat an extremely uninspired home side 2-1. The defeat saw the Latics drop five points behind first placed Sunderland. They clung onto second spot on goal difference alone with third placed Ipswich still very much in contention.

Top of the table Sunderland were up next for the Latics and a 1-0 loss in front of an expectant 20,745 at the JJB saw the club drop to third. Sunderland's eight point lead at the top of the table with five to play would prove unassailable and they'd go on to be crowned worthy champions. Wigan Athletic, however, still had every chance of clawing back the three points it trailed Ipswich. The rewards and untold riches that accession to the Premiership promised demanded that the club leave no stone unturned in the promotion hunt.

Wigan Fans celebrate at the JJB

Dave & Pat Whelan (middle left) watching a match at the JJB

Jewell rallied his troops for the run in and they bounced back to win two on the trot, the latter a victory over seventeenth placed Leicester City with two goals from loan signing Brett Ormerod. Misfiring Latics top scorer Ellington was dropped in favour of the fresh-legged Ormerod in a tactical masterstroke by Jewell who had seen his jaded squad run out of steam at this stage the previous season.

With three games to play Wigan had climbed back into second spot and were three points clear of chasing Ipswich. It was going to go down to the wire. A tense nil-nil draw with mid-table QPR was not the type of result that was going to fire the club to the Premiership and by the time it lined up against fourth placed Preston in the penultimate game of the season, the Latics were two points clear of Ipswich in third. A fiercely fought 1-1 draw at Deepdale condemned Preston to the play-offs and saw Ipswich draw level on points with the Latics. It was too close to call.

The biggest game in Wigan Athletic's history could not have boasted more intrigue had it been scripted by a Hollywood screenwriter. Wigan's opposition for the final match of the season couldn't have been tougher. Reading sat seventh in the league and a win would put them in pole position for the final play-off position. With far superior goal difference to Ipswich, Wigan needed only to match their result with Brighton to guarantee automatic promotion. If the Latics fared worse than Ipswich they would be condemned to third place. Having been so unlucky in recent years in the play-offs everyone at the club knew that they had to be avoided at all costs.

Jewell was unfazed. He was preparing to write his own happy ending to the season:

"I am keyed up inside because I am passionate about the situation," he said in the *Manchester Evening News*. "I simply want the very best for this club. Everyone here at Wigan wants to play in the big games. I want to be in the Premiership and to be playing Manchester United and Liverpool next year.

"I'm asking the players and the fans for one last big effort because they have been superb all season. This is it, this is our big chance. We have enjoyed a great season and have made fantastic progress in a very short period of time. Everything is geared towards this massive game and making sure we do what is expected of us."

As the games at the JJB and at Brighton's Withdean Stadium kicked off simultaneously, the tension in both grounds was palpable. The atmosphere in Lancashire took a serious dip just four minutes in when news filtered through that Ipswich had taken an early lead. As it stood the Latics would finish third. The next 17 minutes would change everything. First Brighton equalised with Ipswich. The Latics were back in second place. Then on eighteen minutes a close range strike from McCulloch at the JJB put the club firmly in the driving seat. Celebrations had barely died down when Roberts scored again three minutes later to seal promotion for the Latics.

Ellington later added a third with his 24th goal of the season to spark wild celebrations. The Latics barely even noticed Steve Sidwell's 90th minute consolation goal. They were already in Premiership dreamland. The Latics were in the top flight for the first time in their history and the biggest party to ever hit the Lancashire town commenced. As the final whistle sounded someone was heard to

Elsewhere in the ground fans unfurled a banner saying, 'Whelan is God'

shout, 'Little Wigan, we're going up!' Elsewhere in the ground fans unfurled a banner saying, 'Whelan is God'. A good-natured pitch invasion followed and widespread euphoria.

One of those to be mobbed by the ecstatic fans was McCulloch. He would be one of the last men standing when the party moved to the town centre later than night. He never doubted that the Latics would do it.

"I'll never forget that day because there was so much hype surrounding the game. We were at home, we needed to win it, it was a sell-out and it was on *Sky Sports*. Ipswich had their game on *Sky* too. I remember in the dressing room and tunnel before the match everybody was so positive. We knew we were going to win. I scored our first goal and it was the best feeling in the world. After the match was brilliant too. To see how together all the squad were was amazing and to see the sheer joy and disbelief on the faces of the fans was great. We went out on the town with them that night. It was a special atmosphere. You wouldn't see that anywhere else. It was an amazing feeling to have achieved that with Wigan."

Jason Roberts also took a great degree of pride from playing his part in the historic promotion.

"We were flying from the moment McCulloch put us ahead," said Roberts to the *Manchester Evening News*. "This was our day, I knew it would be, we were certainly up for it. This is one of my greatest moments in football and I'm just delighted for everyone associated with the club. There's a wonderful spirit at this club and there is no doubting our ambition. It's a truly remarkable success story. When I came to the club I knew this is what we were capable of."

When I came to the club I knew this is what we were capable of

Another man who never doubted his team could clinch automatic promotion was Jewell. If Dave Whelan was God, Jewell was the Lancashire club's answer to Jesus of Nazareth. And Jewell's achievement in the 2004/05 season may just have ranked slightly above the second coming of Christ with Latics fans.

"There's not been a more satisfying moment in my career than when the whistle went against Reading," says Jewell. "The way the staff and players have built Wigan from what it was and grown in the last five years makes me proud to have played my part. To go from 10th in Division Two in my first season to winning the league by 14 points my second, to just missing out on the First Division play-offs to West Ham the following season with the last kick of the season was a real achievement. But to bounce back from that to gain promotion the next season was tremendous. When Chris Hutchings and I came here in 2001 we would never have envisaged that we'd be playing in the Premiership five years later."

It was the stuff of fiction for former player Kenny Morris, who'd seen his Wigan career end just before the club entered the Football League some 27 years earlier.

"After the Reading game I had a tear in my eye. So did a lot of the ex-players who were there that day. There were about 30 of us. We couldn't believe it – Premiership football in Wigan. We were sitting near some fans who had watched the club in the Springfield Park days. You could tell from the looks on their faces how proud they were. Some were crying with joy. You couldn't blame them. The Premiership is the best in the world and Wigan were part of it. It was a fairytale, the stuff of dreams."

It is a sentiment that fellow former player David Hamilton shares:

"I never for one second when I was here as a player thought the club could get into the top flight. Maybe go up to the Championship but never higher. Even with all the money in the world I couldn't see it. Manchester United tried to buy the league for 25 years before finally winning it through hard graft. It's the same here. For a small club like Wigan to be where we are, you pinch yourself. You just couldn't envisage it."

Whelan celebrated side by side with his players, staff and the Latics fans that day. In the heat of the moment he wasn't the wealthy chairman who had ploughed millions into the club. He was a fan, every bit as enthusiastic as that eleven-year-old boy who had starred for Wigan Boys Club alongside Les Campbell so many years before. Even in his moment of triumph Whelan remembered his roots.

"After the match Whelan was surrounded by journalists and photographers but he saw me waiting by the lift in my wheelchair," recalls Campbell. "He pushed away the press and said, 'I just want to have a quick word with Les Campbell'. We spoke about the old days in Wigan and how things had changed. I thought that was a really nice gesture. It showed a human side to him that few outside of the club get to see."

As the party raged on into the night in Wigan, first editions of the following day's newspapers were already landing with a thump on doorsteps all around the country. The chairmen of numerous lower and non-league clubs would read with interest of Wigan Athletic's exploits over their cornflakes. More astute reporters from the broadsheets were already debunking the myth that the Latics had bought promotion to the Premiership. Far from it, Jewell had spent more sparingly than most other teams in the league and had a wage bill that had been only eighth biggest in the entire league.

"It cost us in the region of £3.7m net to go from the Second Division to The Premiership," says Jewell proudly. "I think if you went to any Second Division club and said you'd take them to the top flight in three years for that they would bite your hand off."

Jewell is right. The club is now widely held up as the model for how smaller clubs can, with a modest investment, go all the way to the top flight.

"It goes down in history as something special," says Whelan. "A club like Wigan that's only in the Football League 25 years and qualifies for the Premiership. It says to every team in the land it is possible, it can be done."

Former club auditor Ian Halliwell is in agreement.

"Whelan's money hasn't made that much difference on the field. For example, the midfield that served us well in the Championship had come up from the Second Division. Any people investing into a non-league club will look at Wigan as a template for success."

David Hamilton also refutes claims that Whelan's money was the key factor in the club's renaissance on the park.

"From the chairman down to the tea lady the club is run very professionally and everyone is expected to work hard for the common cause. The likes of Doncaster look at us now and think, 'We want to do it like Wigan'."

It is only fair to give Whelan the last word on this. His allegory sums up the winning formula at Wigan Athletic:

"I believe football is very much like business," he says. "You've got to play to win and you've got to have the right team behind you. You've got to work hard and you've got to earn what you get."

From Brenda Spencer to Director of Football John Benson, from Jewell to Hutchings, Lowe to Hamilton, and from Filan through to McCulloch, Whelan had a club he could be proud of. If there was any justice in the world the entire Wigan Athletic staff, and a few fans to boot, would have joined the players and coaching staff on the plane as they departed for their £100,000 end of season Caribbean jolly. The trip was a reward from the chairman for making his dream become a reality. Reward enough for fans would come soon enough as the club looked forward to its first season in the Premiership. That wasn't just as good as an exotic beach holiday. It was like Christmas and all your birthdays rolled into one.

16 THE PREMIERSHIP AT LAST

After an agonising three month wait the final countdown to Wigan Athletic's first ever season in the Premiership had begun. Never a club to rest on its laurels, marketing drives had seen record numbers of season tickets sold and Paul Jewell had his network of 13 scouts scouring Europe for new additions to his squad. The sale of Nathan Ellington to West Brom for £3m was softened by the arrival of Henri Camara from Wolves for a record £3.1m. Apart from the £500,000 paid for Pascal Chimbona, the £750,000 for Ryan Taylor and the £2m for David Connolly, Jewell stayed true to form and didn't make any extravagant purchases. Arjan De Zeeuw rejoined the club from Portsmouth for an undisclosed fee and goalkeeper Mike Pollit joined from Rotherham for £200,000. Every signing was carefully considered and every player who came in would play their part as the club attempted to fight tooth and nail to defend its Premiership status. To do so would be an achievement every bit as impressive as getting into the top flight in the first place.

The Latics were linked to a lot of good players in the close season but its efforts to bring in proven Premiership quality players were hampered by the fact that the club were the bookies' favourites to go straight back down. It wouldn't be the first time that it had happened to one of the newly promoted teams. As the start of the season neared the club had missed out on a number of transfer targets. For Chris Hutchings it was a source of great frustration:

The club were the bookies' favourites to go straight back down

"When we came up to the Premiership with Sunderland and West Ham we were the last of those clubs that players wanted to come to," says Hutchings. "They had both been established in that league before and were getting 40,000 a week watching them. The only way we could get players to come here was by paying them more but that wasn't the route we wanted to go down."

The result was that the club started the season with the smallest squad in the Premiership. Jewell resisted signing quick fixes and worked tirelessly to get the right sort of player into the club. It made chief scout David Hamilton's job even more difficult.

"We had real problems attracting players and missed out on a lot of people we wanted," says Hamilton. "People think we spent a lot of money but our net outlay for the 2005/06 season was in the region of £5m. Everyone that cost us money did well and if you look at the team who played against Reading in the last game of the season and the team that took the field in the first game in the Premiership there were seven new players. To see them gel together in training in such a short time was a big positive and prove that we were signing the right sort of players."

The prospect of Premiership football caused a sea change behind the scenes at the club. Whereas the club had little income in The Championship and relied on Whelan to bank-roll almost the entire operation, suddenly there was the small matter of £20m from the league's television rights deal coming in. The club had taken an important step towards self-sufficiency. The figures astonished Brenda Spencer who still had the memory of a £5,000 weekly wage bill at the club fresh in her mind.

"At the beginning of the season I was doing the figures for cashflow and I had to start counting the noughts to check that I'd added enough on. It was very daunting at first. The TV money was drastically higher than in The Championship and we'd gone from signing players for £30,000 to signing them for £3m. I sat there sometimes and thought, 'This is ridiculous'. But it was a reflection of our success."

The club's modest expenditure ahead of its first Premiership campaign was the talk of the town during pre-season. It was a fact that had attracted the attention of football pundit Rodney Marsh. Marsh pledged to go to Wigan and be pelted with rotten tomatoes if the Latics avoided relegation that season. Marsh just didn't think they had the personnel:

"I said that if Wigan went up they would go straight back down. I said that because, in my view, they're simply not good enough to survive. I was under the impression that Wigan were set to spend £25m to establish themselves in the Premiership, yet, up to now they have spent only £3m."

Only time would tell if Jewell knew what he was doing. One man convinced that he did was Arjan De Zeeuw.

"I'd kept in contact with Paul throughout my time at Portsmouth," says the Dutchman. "He'd made me aware that he'd take me back if they'd let me go. It wasn't a hard decision to come back but it was a gamble because Wigan were favourites to go back down. I was confident we could prove everyone wrong though. It was strange coming back but everything had changed. The club had moved up a notch. The first thing I noticed was in the town centre. When I first played here everyone would walk around the town centre in rugby tops. By the time I came back there were probably more Wigan Athletic football tops."

Though everyone at the club secretly dreamed of a top ten finish in the Premiership, an air of pragmatism prevailed. Staying in the league would be an astonishing feat, especially as the backbone of the squad was largely unchanged from the one that won promotion. Lee McCulloch, who was looking forward to playing in the Premiership for the first time was under no illusions about the difficulty of the task ahead.

"We knew the first year was going to be tough. We had a small squad, many of whom had never played in the top flight before, and we were going into the best league in the world. Getting there was incredible but the pressure was now on for us to stay there."

Hutchings joined McCulloch in his assessment of the job at hand. Having kept Bradford in the Premiership in their first season up with Jewell he knew what a mammoth task it was.

"Our aspirations for the first season were simple: survival. We never kidded ourselves that we'd be up at the top challenging for the title. We were realistic. Alongside probably 14 other clubs we just wanted to stay in the league. That was the priority."

Ever since the Latics had been promoted there was huge anticipation about who their first Premiership opponents would be. All fans look forward to receiving the new fixture list but this was a whole new ball game. Never before had the fans been able to look forward to world class players like Rooney, Gerrard, and Henry gracing the JJB. When the season's fixtures were issued a collective intake of breath was audible in the Lancashire town. The Latics first game of the season pitched them against champions Chelsea at the JJB. The club couldn't have asked for a tougher initiation.

Expectations had reached fever pitch by the time Chelsea arrived in the town on August 14. A record 23,575 filled the JJB to watch the newcomers take on the princes of the Premiership. The atmosphere was electric at the stadium for the club's first Premiership tie and the game fittingly went down to the wire. On 90 minutes still no-one had broken the deadlock and a well-earned point looked to be coming the Latics' way. In truth they'd had enough chances to win the match. It would be a baptism of fire for the club, however. Just as they were resigned to a draw, substitute Hernan Crespo advanced on goal and struck an unstoppable drive past Mike Pollitt. It was a sign of how far the club had come that the fans could feel disgruntled conceding a last minute winner from Argentina's number one striker, one of the best strikers in the world, playing for one of the best teams in the world.

The match-up between the Premiership new boys and the newly crowned champions, managed by the precocious José Mourinho, put the Latics firmly on the radar of the national press. The media had first started to take notice of the Latics late the previous season when it looked like they were destined for promotion. Wigan Athletic media manager Matt McCann recalls how attitudes to the club and the town changed as the Latics established themselves in the Premiership:

"When I was still a journalist during the 2004/05 promotion season my colleagues and I would play Wigan Cliché Bingo. Whenever the club was mentioned in the nationals we'd read the article looking for references to pies, flat caps, whippets, Wigan Pier, George Formby, George Orwell, and rugby league. We'd go tick, tick, tick and say 'full house' when we'd spotted them all. It doesn't happen now. They've started talking about the great football story here."

The coverage wasn't limited just to the UK press. It showed how far the club had come and how far news of its amazing progress up the leagues had travelled when Arab news station Al Jazeera visited Wigan to do a report on the club. During their first season in the Premiership, journalists from as far afield as Japan and Australia travelled to the JJB while *BBC Five Live* followed the team for the season and a US television crew made a fly-on-the-wall documentary.

Wigan's last minute heartache to Chelsea dominated the back pages of every British newspaper the following morning. Despite the disappointment, the club took great strength from the fact that they had held their own against the best team in the league. There was every cause for optimism as the Latics travelled to Charlton the following Saturday. A 1-0 loss at The Valley was a rude awakening for the Latics, however. It's a match they'd identified before the season started as one they could take some points from. With only two games played, Matt Jackson was already viewing the club's next fixture against Sunderland at home as a relegation six-pointer.

"We got a bit of a drubbing at Charlton. Our next game was Sunderland at

Dave Whelan with Sir Alex Ferguson during a match against Manchester United

home and even that early in the season we knew that was a make or break match. I maintain that if we hadn't won that day we could have found the roles would be reversed with Sunderland who went down that season."

The Latics edged the tight game 1-0 to pick up their first points of the season. It was a massive confidence boost to Jewell's inexperienced squad. Two defeats on the trot had left many behind the scenes and on the terraces questioning Wigan's Premiership pedigree. But as it had done so many times before, the club bounced back stronger from adversity. The win over the Wearsiders sparked an eleven game unbeaten run in cup and league, including eight wins in a row – six in the league – when the Latics didn't concede a single goal. After beating Fulham 1-0 on October 29, the club hit second spot in the league behind Chelsea. It was an incredible feat and one that was thought unimaginable at the outset of the season.

Jackson puts the club's improving league position down to the confidence the Latics drew from a Carling Cup (League Cup) run that had seen them beat Bournemouth, Watford, Newcastle and Bolton without conceding a goal.

"We knew the Premiership was going to be tough but there was never a feeling amongst the players that we were going to come back down. Something which is overlooked is that we had a good cup run early in the season where we had beaten a number of Premiership clubs. So when we got round to facing them in the league we weren't particularly fazed."

The lengthy cup run soon left the small matter of Arsene Wenger's Arsenal as the only obstacle between the Latics and a trip to the final at the Millennium Stadium. The League Cup semi beckoned in the New Year. It was still November and it would be Arsenal, ironically, that would bring the Latics unbeaten league run to an end. The battling 3-2 defeat in front of 25,004 at the JJB saw the club drop to third in the league. The Latics were still riding high. Indeed, having been in the top ten since the fourth game of the Premiership campaign the club would not drop outside it again the entire season. The cushion that the early season run of form brought was a critical element in the club's survival that season.

"We just wanted to get 40 points," says Chris Hutchings. "So when we went up to the top of the table it was fantastic. It also meant that even if we lost three or four on the trot we wouldn't drop below mid-table. That was a huge psychological boost. It was vital."

Hutchings wouldn't have known just how vital at the time. The Latics loss at the hands of Arsenal marked the start of a slump where the club were beaten back-to-back by the eventual top five clubs in the league: Arsenal, Tottenham, Liverpool, Chelsea and Manchester United. The ominous 4-0 loss to Man Utd on December 14 saw the club drop to eighth in the table. Jewell and Hutchings refused to panic.

"After we lost against all the big guns we were still above halfway in the table," says Hutchings. "They were the best teams in the league so we didn't panic and let it cloud our judgement. We decided to look at the performances in those games even if we were getting beat."

The young management team's cool approach seemed to work. The club responded to win its next four matches. As the New Year dawned, the Latics had climbed up to fifth. It would be good enough for a UEFA Cup place if it could be maintained and would have been a huge upset. In the December run Whelan's old club Blackburn visited the JJB. It was an emotional occasion for Whelan

To show some festive good cheer he offered all Blackburn fans a free pie

and he decided to show some festive good cheer by offering all Blackburn fans a free pie at half time. As Ian Halliwell recalls, the gesture caused outrage with Latics fans:

"The Wigan fans were in uproar so Whelan said they'd get their pies half price. On match day in the away end there are usually two windows open in the shop with four serving. For Blackburn he had one window open with one selling. No-one could get a pie! That's typical Whelan."

Latics fans would forgive their chairman almost anything at that time, however. They were in the top six as the year came to a close and had a Carling Cup semi final with Arsenal to look forward to. Having not conceded in the competition to date, the Latics were relishing the visit of the Gunners for the semi-final first leg. It was a typically tense affair that could have gone either way but against the odds Jewell's injury ravaged squad edged the match 1-0 with a goal from substitute and debutant Paul Scharner late in the match.

The stage was set for a classic return leg at Highbury and, with Chelsea dominating the league, Arsene Wenger would field a first choice squad in the hope of reaching the first major final of the year. 3,000 Latics fans made the journey to London for the match and they wouldn't be disappointed. After seeing Pollitt save a José Reyes penalty early in the first half, Thiery Henry

Above: Fireworks and ticker-tape at Highbury for the final match at the Arsenal stadium, against Wigan

Below: A Highbury market stall on the day of last game of the season and the last game at Highbury

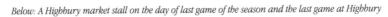

finally found the net for the gunners on 65 minutes. With the scores level on aggregate, the matched moved into extra time. Mid-way through the second period of extra time Henry's replacement Robin Van Persie seemed to have settled the tie with a free kick. Jason Roberts clearly hadn't read the script. With just a minute remaining he latched onto a Grahmam Kavanagh through ball and slotted the ball past Mañuel Almunia to level the tie.

When the final whistle sounded just moments later many inside the ground, not least Whelan, assumed penalties would ensue. Brenda Spencer knew better:

"Hand on heart, going into the game I couldn't see us beating Arsenal to reach the final. I was sitting next to the chairman and his wife. When the whistle went I jumped straight up and Dave said, 'Sit down woman, we've got penalties'. I said, 'No, we're through on away goals'. He jumped up too and was jubilant. It was great, everyone was on such a high."

Pollitt who was the Latics hero that night was also unsure of whether there'd be a penalty shoot-out.

"It was the game of my life and I didn't realise we'd gone through straightaway, I was preparing for penalties as I'd completely forgotten about the away-goals rule. Then I saw the chairman dancing on the pitch and I knew we'd done it. The fairytale continued."

Jewell revelled in the victory too.

"I don't like to show my emotion too much but I couldn't help myself at the end. I thought the players deserved it and we were fantastic. We had three penalties turned down, saved one. Getting to the Premiership was the best thing we've ever done. Staying in the Premiership will be even better, but that was a nice bonus."

One player who was not there to join the celebrations was the squad's longest serving player, Lee McCulloch. But the Scotsman, who was recovering from a double hernia operation in hospital, felt far from left out.

"I was lying in a hospital bed that night watching the semi-final and was pretty miserable but Jason Roberts scored in the last minute and he and Jimmy Bullard ran up to one of the cameramen and were shouting my name down the camera. That was a special moment and summed up the spirit of the squad. They knew I'd be suffering."

The Carling Cup final was another historic first for the club. It was a massive addition to Jewell's already impressive managerial CV. If he could pull off an unexpected victory over opponents Manchester United in the final it would be an achievement on a par with Wimbledon's 1988 FA Cup success following their climb up the leagues in the 1980s. There were many parallels between Wimbledon and Wigan Athletic. Latics' fans hoped, however, that their rise to the top would not be followed by a plummet down the table like their southern counterparts had recently suffered.

Wigan Athletic in the Carling Cup Final. It was hard to take in for most fans. The season which some fans had approached with trepidation was proving to be the most memorable on record. 27,000 Latics fans would make the journey down to Cardiff for the first major final in the club's history. It was more than had ever gone to the JJB at any one time. Spencer would not have missed the game for the world.

Wigan in the Carling Cup Final. It was hard to take in for most fans

"I'd booked a holiday to Egypt for when the Carling Cup Final was on never dreaming for a minute that we'd be there. I had to cancel the trip to go to the final. I never had a moment's hesitation. My friends that I was supposed to go on holiday with could not understand why I couldn't miss the game. I couldn't explain it to them but it was never an option after all I'd been through with the club. I'm glad I never missed it because everything about the build-up was great: the interest from the press and fans, the walk to the stadium, the atmosphere on the day. Everyone made the most of it because you never know when that will happen again."

Though expectation of a first major cup victory was high, no fan who travelled to Cardiff that day could quite get the memory of the 4-0 defeat they'd suffered at the hands of Man Utd earlier in the season out of their heads. It had been the best football the JJB had seen all season as Rooney, Ronaldo *et al* ran riot. The prospect of a repeat performance scared the living daylights out of the Latics fans.

The fears were well-founded. For the first time in recent memory the Latics performed well below par and bore no resemblance to the combative, disciplined unit that had done so well in the league that year. Jewell's team was never in the game and the 4-0 defeat was the biggest final loss in League Cup history. It's an experience Jewell won't quickly forget.

"I didn't enjoy the final," says Jewell. "You have to accept getting beaten in football but maybe I picked the wrong team. If I had my time again I'd

Above & below:
The Carling Cup Final at The Millennium Stadium

The Premiership At Last

Chris Hutchings

definitely pick a different team. I have to take responsibility for that but the team I picked should have done better than they did. We gave a bad goal away before half-time and missed a good chance just after. We never really showed our true colours. If we'd gone and played somewhere near out potential and lost we could have accepted that. When we were getting beaten 4-0 with 20 minutes to go I was thinking, 'This is not a nice experience'. But we've had that experience and we'll learn from it and if we get the chance to go back there hopefully we can do better."

Whelan, who by this time had put the better part of £60m into the club, was more philosophical in the face of defeat:

"It was a great occasion for our club and to see all those supporters in the stadium was brilliant. At the start of the season, if someone had offered me a place in the Carling Cup final and said we would lose, I would have taken it. Of course, once you get there and it happens, it's disappointing to say the least. We are down, but we won't be down for long and we will learn from this."

Whelan was being premature. The squad didn't immediately take many positives from losing so badly in their first major final.

"It was disappointing to go to Cardiff and not perform professionally on the day," says Matt Jackson. "It was the pinnacle of the season for the fans and the players but after the disappointment of being beaten we were never really the same team after it."

In retrospect, it's clear that the Carling Cup run did cause the Latics league form to suffer. In the time between their semi-final success on January

24 and the final on February 26 the club hadn't won a league game and had dropped from sixth to tenth in the Premiership. During that period it had also been knocked out of the FA Cup by Manchester City. The club's last win in the league had been against Middlesborough on January 21. It was to get worse. From then to the season-end the Latics would only win three of its 15 games. A February 11 loss to Liverpool saw the Latics drop out of the European places for good.

Jackson singles out the Middlesborough game as the point when the end of season malaise started.

"Getting 40 points and staying up was our realistic target that year but when we found ourselves in the top six at Christmas we felt that it was going to be easily achievable. We got to 37 points after beating Boro away and the lads knew then that we were going to be okay. The hard work was done and that might have been a contributing factor to the end of season slump too.

"There was never a feeling of slackening off but some of the players who'd played a lot of matches were getting tired because playing in the Premiership was a whole new challenge for the squad, both physically and mentally. Teams visiting the JJB were giving us more respect too and strangely that made it harder to pick up points. We cruised over the 40 points in the end but it did take us longer than expected."

The Latics finally hit the magical 40 points with 11 games to spare after a draw with Tottenham on Feb 19, 2006. Regardless of the club's great start to the season, it was a remarkable achievement for the newly promoted side. The club would end the season on 51 points in tenth place – an astounding result in a season where the club had simply hoped to avoid the drop. Instead they'd consolidated in style, spending nearly half the season in the European qualification places. They'd end up 12 points shy of the UEFA Cup places but there was no cause for complaint. It was just a case of what could have been. Jewell couldn't have been prouder of the team, many of whom had been with him since the early days of the adventure.

Playing in the Premiership and finishing top ten is nothing less than a dream

"There were too many highlights to count that season. From the first televised game against Chelsea at the JJB to the last game of the season at

Highbury, which was the last ever game at the ground, it was nothing short of a fairytale."

Hutchings is in agreement:

"We were written off straightaway at the start of the season and it was great to prove people wrong. All credit to the players because lots of them hadn't played in the top flight before we got in. We laid down the gauntlet and they picked it up and proved they were good enough. Finishing 10th in the league alone would have been unbelievable but to go on a cup run to the final was the icing on the cake. It was fantastic for the fans. It was great to see the top teams at the JJB Stadium but to go to the Millennium Stadium to play Manchester United was what you go into the game for."

Alex Cribley has nothing but respect for what Jewell and Hutchings achieved:

"When you look at what Paul and Chris have done, you have to ask yourself could an established senior manager and coach have done it any better. I don't think they could. To get two promotions in quick succession, survive your first year in the Premiership and finish in the top half of the table, and get to a major final is just unbelievable. If you'd told anyone in Wigan five years ago that that was what was in store they would have thought you were crazy. If you stopped to think about where we are and where we've come from it's pretty scary."

Former Latics manager Ian McNeill is also full of praise for what the club has achieved.

"To be playing in the Premiership and finishing in the top ten is nothing less than a dream come true."

With Wigan Athletic having been in the top half of the season for much of the season, it is easy to be blasé about the magnitude of what the club achieved in the 2005/06 season. It was an astonishing feat for a club that came within a whisker of going out of business just ten years before.

Detractors will point out that the club has a particularly rich benefactor who has gifted them a £25m stadium and pumped millions into the club along the way but we've already dispelled the myth that the club bought success. Football is not as easy as that – see Chelsea's failed European campaigns in the early Abramovich era as a case in point.

Far from buying success, the ten year climb up the leagues that followed Whelan's takeover was faltering though, retrospectively, swift. The club struggled. It learnt that throwing money at a problem does not solve it. Not for one minute can it be suggested that it could have been done without Dave Whelan's generosity but it may also never have been done without Jewell, Hutchings and the many players and staff that lent their weight to the cause. And let's not forget the fans who put £10 notes into collection buckets week in week out for years to pay the players' wages or the procession of well-meaning but poorly funded chairmen who fought tooth and nail to keep the club afloat throughout the 1970s, 1980s and 1990s. They all played their part in making sure the club lived to see the success it now enjoys.

Last but by no means least let us not forget the hardy forefathers of Wigan Athletic who can be traced all the way back to the late 1800s. If it wasn't for their bloody-minded persistence the 'dribbling game' would never have taken a foothold in the town in the first place. In light of the events of the last few years the prospect is something which is frankly unimaginable.

Dave and Pat Whelan

EPILOGUE

It has been a rollercoaster ride for Wigan Athletic Football Club. Not just in their first season in the top flight when they held their own against some of the best football teams on the planet. Nor in their second Premiership campaign when they showed grit and determination to avoid the drop with a last gasp win on the final day of the season. And not just in the last ten years, which have seen the Latics bounce back from the very foot of the Football League to the very pinnacle of the game. No. The ups and downs have spanned the club's entire history.

Since 1932 Wigan Athletic have gone from non-league giant to Football League hopeful; from League hopeful to trophy winners at Wembley; and, from trophy winners back down to League strugglers, languishing on the bottom rung of the Football League ladder. From that moment until the present it has been the stuff of fairytale. Millions or no millions, to go from 92nd to, at one point, 2nd in the Football League in ten years is nothing short of extraordinary.

Now Wigan Athletic face a whole new challenge. The club must guard against ever ending up in a position where it may crash down the leagues again. As the disappointing 2006/07 season proved, that challenge never stops. But they must keep rallying. For, if the club can stay in the Premiership, it will benefit from a television rights windfall that could see it free forever of reliance on the blessing and burden that is Dave Whelan's wealth. The new deal, which commenced at the start of the 2007/08 season, saw the club earn at least £30m from TV rights alone. It is a dizzying figure and no one at the club is more aware of the importance of the club sticking around to reap the benefits than club chief executive Brenda Spencer.

"It costs a lot of money to run a football club and anybody who tells you that they're in football to make money is lying," says Spencer. "But if we can stay in the Premiership then we can be self-financing with TV money and money from the league alone. It's that simple."

Spencer's prediction is supported by Dan Brown, Partner in Sports Business Group at Deloitte, publishers of the *Annual Review of Football Finance*:

"The revenue boost which the Premiership provides is, if invested wisely, sufficient for a promoted (recently) club to achieve survival."

The significance of this drive to self-finance should not be underplayed. Every Latics fan over the age of 30 remembers the pre-Whelan era. It seems light years away, like a different lifetime, compared to fortunes the club is enjoying as it goes about consolidating its place at football's top table. What no one can predict, and what no fans or people at the club dare even consider, is what will happen in the post-Whelan era. With heir apparent Duncan Sharpe sadly no longer with us it is the most commonly asked question at the club's AGM. It is a question that Paul Jewell even asked of Whelan during his time with the club.

"What happens after Whelan was obviously a difficult subject to broach," says Jewell. "I asked him what will happen to the club if anything happens to him and he said there is money that's in trust for the club."

Whelan's philosophy on how to spend his incredible wealth will be of comfort to some fans:

"I do not want to be the richest man in the graveyard," says Whelan. "Too many people go to their graves having left millions of pounds behind – what use is that? It is much better invested in football and sport rather than having the government grab their 40 per cent. I'm damn glad my money is in sport and is being enjoyed by the people of Wigan."

Spencer is quick to point out that there are any number of the Whelan family who may step into the chairman's shoes in the future:

Dave loves football and I think his family will keep the tradition going

"Dave's wife, his daughter and his two grandsons all come to every Wigan Athletic game and are very keen fans. Dave loves football and I think his family will keep the tradition going if anything happens to him and will follow his wish, which is to back the club. There are generations coming through who will hopefully be involved with the club for a long time to come. Dave has also sorted out a trust. It's a private arrangement between Dave and the club. The closest thing I can liken it to is the Jack Walker situation at Blackburn. Walker invested a lot of time and money in Blackburn and when he died he left a trust in place and the club is his legacy for the people of Blackburn. It's the same at Wigan. I'm satisfied that the trust combined with the continued interest of the Whelan family will bode well for the club in the future."

Most Latics fans do not live in fear of the future, however. They are an optimistic bunch but are pragmatic to a man. None more so than lifelong fan and former journalist, Harold Ashurst.

"If it all comes crashing down tomorrow we've enjoyed the ride and we'll pick up the pieces and start again."

It will be a relief to most fans, however, to hear that plans are in place to secure the long-term future of the club they love. Nick Bitel airs a valid word of caution, however:

"Post-Whelan, unless things have radically changed at the club someone is going to have to put some money in. Even if there is a trust fund someone has to fund losses."

There's wisdom in what Bitel says but he may underestimate the work that is being done behind the scenes at the club. In addition to the millions the club receives from TV rights, it is also starting to realise a decent chunk of revenue from the turnstiles. The average attendance in the 2005/06 season was 20,904. For a club in a town of 90,000 people, a club that used to struggle to get 1,500, that has Bolton Wanderers, Blackburn Rovers, Manchester United, Liverpool and Everton to name but a few within a 20 mile radius of its stadium, it is nothing short of remarkable. And although TV revenue far surpasses that taken on the gate at the JJB, those within the club view the latter as the real key to their future survival.

"I doubt that average crowds at Wigan will ever go below 8,000 again," says Matt McCann. "It doesn't sound like much but if I'd said that ten years ago people would have laughed at me. To get an average gate of over 20,000 is phenomenal. We want to get as many of them as possible to become what we'd call proper football fans who come every time we play, no matter what league it is or who we're playing against. That is a philosophy that runs right through the club from Dave Whelan down.

"I think we've got a solid fan-base now that will follow the club more passionately than any other generation of Wiganers. The biggest contributing factor to that is the work that's been done over the last seven years to build up the junior support. Going forward this club will have generations of fans that it could never have dreamt of ten years ago. We have 4,000 kids who come to every game now. Because of this, whoever is chief executive of the club in 15 years time will never have to face the same problems that Brenda Spencer did during the club's dark days."

But this isn't a time for doom and gloom and uncertainty. This is a time to rejoice if you're a Latic. At the time of writing there is a third season of Premiership football to look forward too. As the club faces up to challenges off the pitch so too must the manager and players on it because the task ahead is an onerous one. Wigan Athletic are far from entrenched in the league and the difficulty of maintaining the club's Premiership status in an ever-more-competitive league should not be underestimated. It's a fact known only too well by Paul Jewell who stepped down as manager after a nervy run-in in the 2006/07 season saw the club preserve its Premiership status on the very last day of the campaign.

"Whether it's me that's manager or someone else, this club will not rest on its laurels," said Jewell. "The club might not finish better than 10th or go to a cup final again soon but the priority is to consolidate in the Premiership. In the 2005/06 season everyone thought that we were going to be like the Christmas decorations – going down before the New Year – but that season is gone. Wigan have to be better every season. All the staff have to be better, to work harder. The club has to bring in better players and make sure that players they've already got play better."

Jewell's successor in the managerial hot seat, Chris Hutchings, shared his caution as he looked forward to his first season in charge:

"We've stayed up twice but the hardest thing is doing it again and again. That's another challenge. You need the right players, the right management, the right money behind you but it can be done."

The importance and difficulty of making the club a permanent fixture in the top flight is never far from the minds of the players either, as Latics' legend Matt Jackson says:

"There are three teams coming up every season who are going to be facing what we did in 2005/06. That is why it is important for the club to establish itself as quickly as possible to secure its future in the division."

The Latics' backroom staff share the view.

"No-one will ever get complacent here and think that because we're in the Premiership we've arrived," says Alex Cribley. "What we did in our first season up could be done at anytime by the three new clubs coming up, putting pressure on clubs like Wigan."

David Hamilton was brutally honest when he spoke on the topic ahead of the 2006/07 season. His assessment of the task ahead proved to be alarmingly accurate.

A line-up of former Wigan players

"I'd take 17th position in the league if you offered it to me now," said Hamilton in August 2006. "Yes we expect better but we'd take it because we've got to stay in this league at all costs. You only have to look at Birmingham who were considered one of the established teams to see how easy it is to slip out of the top flight. We have to work harder to match what we did in our first season up. And that is everybody involved in the club from players through to staff."

Those on the outside looking in, like former manager Bruce Rioch, are less cautious about the club's chances of surviving in the top flight.

"Wigan should do okay in the long term. They've had one good and one disappointing season in the Premiership but they've survived, which is the main thing, and the experience should stand them in good stead. They really need to establish themselves now and that should be helped by them having more buying power than the clubs coming up."

Despite having the not inconsiderable wealth of Dave Whelan behind them, the club does still miss out on many of its signing targets, however. This is because it is still viewed as a small club by Premiership standards. The Latics' summer signings in 2006 were, however, the biggest statement yet that this is a club that had arrived in the upper echelons of the game and doesn't plan to go anywhere soon. Joining Wigan Athletic's squad in the 2006 close season were England internationals Emile Heskey (for a club record £5.5m) and Chris Kirkland, Dutch international Denny Landzaat (for a fee in the

Above & below:
The JJB Stadium

region of £2.5m), Ecuador midfielder Antonio Valencia (loan), and talented Crystal Palace defensive duo Fitz Hall (£3m) and Emerson Boyce (for a fee in the region of £1m).

Jewell balanced the books with the reluctant sale of, amongst others, Jimmy Bullard to Fulham for £2.5m, Pascal Chimbonda to Tottenham for £6m, Jason Roberts to Blackburn for a mooted fee of £2.2m, and Damien Francis to Watford for £1.5m. Based on disclosed figures, far from having a high close season spend, the club recorded a net profit of £600,000 in its dealings in the transfer market. Some fans would have been happier if the club had spent more but most trusted Jewell's judgement on the matter. The young manager had taken a great deal of pride in attracting such an array of international talent to the club.

"The Emile Heskey deal shows our intentions," said Jewell at the time. "He is the most high-profile signing this club has ever made and it is a major coup for us. I have said all along I want to bring real quality performers into this club and Emile fits into that category. It shows that we can attract top talent."

The young manager had no trouble getting quality players like Kirkland to buy into his vision of the future for Wigan.

"I sat down with Paul Jewell ahead of the 2006/07 season and he told me how ambitious the club was," says Kirkland. "That sealed it for me."

Fitz Hall, too, took little persuasion to join Whelan's ambitious squad.

"After seeing the club in the 2005/06 season I couldn't wait to join," says Hall. "I admired what they had achieved and could see that they are a club that wants to keep on bettering itself."

And that is the aim at the club, as confirmed by Jewell ahead of the 2006/07 season:

After seeing the club last season I couldn't wait to join

"We don't want to be 'little Wigan'. We're trying to build something sustainable here. If we can remain in the Premiership for the next three years then I think we can consider ourselves established there. That is going to be very, very difficult but it's something that with the right players I think we can achieve. If we can stay in the division for the next few seasons it will be massive for this club. Maybe we can even start competing with the bigger clubs for honours."

When Chris Hutchings took the helm at the end of the 2006/07 season he found that Dave Whelan was in accord with Jewell. Further, the chairman had already set his sights on a new target altogether.

"The chairman's dream at one stage was to get the club into the Premiership. We've done that now so we need a new dream. That has to be Europe. Who's to say we can't do it?"

It's thinking outside of the box like this that enabled Wigan Athletic to rise out of the ashes to become a Premiership side in the first place. Who would bet against them going on to achieve Whelan's next dream of seeing European football played at the JJB?

Much to the chagrin of fans and colleagues alike, that's a journey that will be taken without Jewell. Indeed, there are many who have found it hard to adjust to a Wigan Athletic without the popular manager. His work ethic, honesty and down-to-earth demeanour were emblematic of the football club. That coda will be part of the fabric of the club for years to come. It is the very bedrock on which Wigan Athletic as we know it is built. But with Jewell gone it is up to Whelan to keep providing the support; to Hutchings (and subsequent managers) to turn that support to the club's advantage; to the fans to keep coming through the turnstiles; and to the players and staff at the club to make sure that Wigan Athletic becomes a club capable of competing at the highest level.

This brings us to the end of this sprint through the history of Wigan Athletic FC. As the club embarks on the most exciting period in its history there is no doubt that its story will run and run. When Dave Whelan took over at Springfield Park the club changed forever but who is to say that they wouldn't have dragged themselves up by the bootlaces and achieved what they have anyway? For it is a club quite unlike any other. It lately has the face of a big business but retains the heart and spirit of an even bigger family. It is the second team of everyone that knows them, not as Paul Jewell once said, "Because their first team always beat us!" but because it is a decent, honest, humble football club that will never forget where it has come from.

The club knows its history because most of it has been so vividly stark and bleak. Because of that, fans and staff and people like the late Ken Cowap, who would have given the last shilling from his slot machine empire if it meant the club would see another day, deserve more than anyone to see Wigan Athletic prosper. This is their time. These are Wigan Athletic's halcyon days.

As Dave Whelan says, "Wigan have made it!"

Latics beat Fulham away, 2006-07 season

ACKNOWLEDGEMENTS

I would like to thank the following:

Harold Ashurst; Graham Barrow; Nick Bitel; Les Campbell; Ken Cowap; Alfie Craig; Alex Cribley; Mike & Tricia Davies; John Deehan; Lara Ellsworth-Jones; Stephen Gage; Tommy Gore; Ian Halliwell (Rik); Bryan Hamilton; David Hamilton; Richard Hatherall; Chris Hutchings; Matt Jackson; Billy Lomax; David Lowe; Ray Mathias; Ian McNeill; Lee McCulloch; Kenny Morris; Bernard Ramsdale (www.yeoldetreeandcrown.34sp.com); Bruce Rioch; Tommy Ross; Brenda Spencer; Virgin Trains; Amy Wadsworth; Wigan Observer

Last but not least Dave Whelan, Paul Jewell and Wigan Athletic Football Club without whom this book could not have been written. Special thanks also to Matt McCann for giving me unlimited access to the club and for permission to reproduce photographs from the club archive.

All photographs courtesy of Wigan Athletic excluding
p.23 (top) ©Kemsley Newspapers; p.33 ©Tommy Ross; p.34 (top) ©Tommy Ross; p.34 (bottom) ©Wigan Observer; p.36 ©Wigan Observer; p.67 ©Wigan Observer; p.82 ©Lancashire Evening Post; p.95 ©Lancashire Evening Post; p.112 ©Derek Davies

Other titles from
Dewi Lewis Media

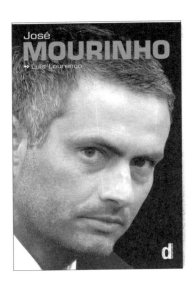

JOSÉ MOURINHO
MADE IN PORTUGAL

the authorised biography
by Luís Lourenço

£12.99 softback
224 pages
ISBN: 0-9546843-3-8

José Mourinho arrived in London in the summer of 2004. The Chelsea manager made an immediate, and at times controversial, impact on English football, with his unmistakeable self-confidence, drive and ambition.

This fascinating book charts his rise from relatively humble beginnings as assistant coach to Sir Bobby Robson, to become the most sought-after club manager in Europe.

Readers will gain an insight into Mourinho's management skills, as well as his whole footballing philosophy, and his approach to motivating his players. Mourinho himself writes of his move to Roman Abramovich's Chelsea and of approaches by other clubs; his 'mind games' with Sir Alex Ferguson as Manchester United are knocked out of Europe; and his fears for his personal safety and that of his family after receiving a death threat on the eve of what should have been the biggest night of his life.

Long-term family friend, Portuguese journalist Luís Lourenço guides us through the formative years in Mourinho's coaching career, as he returns to Portugal from Barcelona at the turn of the millennium and embarks on the remarkable four-year journey which would lead him to Chelsea. A journey which included short-lived yet turbulent spells at Portuguese giants Benfica and minnows União de Leiria, and culminated in a night of unforgettable glory for FC Porto and José Mourinho as they were crowned Champions of Europe.

www.dewilewismedia.com

RAFA BENÍTEZ

the authorised biography
by Paco Lloret

£12.99 softback
224 pages
ISBN: 0-9546843-7-0

On May 25th 2005, Liverpool FC won the Champions League Final in one of the most memorable and extraordinary nights of English football.

This authorised biography of the Liverpool manager is a vivid and lively account of both his personal and professional life, from childhood right through to his current achievements with Liverpool. A talented footballer, Rafa Benítez progressed through the ranks of the Real Madrid youth teams before suffering a serious injury which destroyed his dream of playing at the top of European football. Instead he had to settle for a modest playing career in the lower divisions, but still determined to achieve success in the game he became a coach, initially with Real Madrid's youth teams. Later, as a manager, he took Extremadura and Tenerife to the Spanish first division, before moving to Valencia where he won two League titles and the UEFA Cup. When Liverpool appointed him in June 2004 it was against stiff competition from three other major European clubs.

Lloret gives a real insight into what motivates Benítez, his attention to detail, his man-mangement skills, his sharp football mind and his constant quest to develop the skills of himself and his players. We also discover the steely determination with which he faced his early setbacks, his personal trauma at the tragic death of his brother-in-law, his public anger after the Madrid bombings, and the complex intrigue at Valencia which led to his move to Liverpool.

Paco Lloret has been a sports journalist for over twenty years. He first met Benítez through a mutual friend, journalist Emilio García Carrasco, and this has given him a privileged position from which to explore the personality and achievements of the manager who led Liverpool to European glory in the Champions League.

PRAWNS IN THE GAME

HOW FOOTBALL GOT WHERE IT IS TODAY!

Paul French

£9.99 softback
224 pages, 230mm x 150mm
ISBN: 0-9546843-8-9

Something grotesque is going on in the beautiful game. Money rather than sport now rules the roost. Stadium names are sold off to the highest bidder and players often seem no more than overpaid and over-sexed celebrities. Their every action, both on and off the pitch, is fodder for the tabloids as the players themselves argue over whether it's £100k or £120k a week in their pay packets.

Paul French has talked to leading football pundits as well as to fans from clubs all over the country. Whether they're Reds or Blues they share one thing in common: they're sick and tired of the greed that seems to run through the game they love. They're tired of big businesses slapping their names and logos everywhere, and they hate seeing footballers earn more in a week than they do in a year, particularly when they struggle to even afford the rising admission charge to matches.

Prawns in The Game is the book those fans will need to read to understand how football has ended up where it is today. From the formation of the very first football club to the creation of Arsenal's Emirates stadium, *Prawns in the Game* tells the fascinating story.

This is the only book about the commercialisation of the game written by a fan for the fans. You'll laugh, you'll get angry and you'll find out: how did the prawn sandwich brigade take over the national sport?

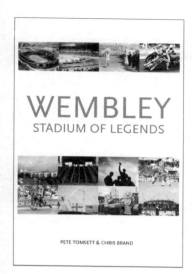

WEMBLEY
STADIUM OF LEGENDS

Pete Tomsett & Chris Brand

£12.99 hardback
160 pages
ISBN: 9780954684396

Everywhere in the world people know of Wembley. Pelé called it the Church of Football and for decades Wembley held pride of place amongst the world's top venues – home to over 200 England internationals, including England's 1966 World Cup victory, 72 F.A. Cup Finals, Euro '96. But Wembley was never just about football. From its early days onwards it has hosted many other sports and events. In fact, sixteen different sports have taken place there at one time or another; it was also home to the 1948 Olympic Games and to Live Aid in 1985, as well as to countless major concerts.

By the 1990s the Stadium of Legends had begun to show its age, and as the new millennium began, Wembley embarked on a major transformation. A magnificent new stadium has now risen from the rubble of the old. With its spectacular arch, the new building is a dramatic addition to the London skyline.

Naturally, *Wembley: Stadium Of Legends* is a book of two halves. It begins with Wembley's extraordinary history – not just football but every aspect – combining remarkable archive images with fascinating information: tales of enigmatic entrepreneurs and entertainers, courageous athletes and odds-defying sportsmen. Through unique photographs, the later chapters tell of the transition from old to new, from the faded grandeur of the old stadium, through its demolition, especially the heartbreaking destruction of the twin towers, to the construction of the new building and its dramatic arch.

The book finishes with a full listing of all the football matches that have ever been played at Wembley, as well as all Rugby League Challenge Cups, World Speedway Championships and concerts.

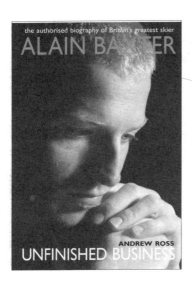

ALAIN BAXTER

UNFINISHED BUSINESS

the authorised biography
by Andrew Ross

£12.99 softback
224 pages
ISBN: 0-9546843-5-4

Alain Baxter is Britain's leading skier – the only Briton to have ever won a Winter Olympics medal in the history of the Games. Nicknamed 'The Highlander" he is a one-off, the greatest skier Britain has ever produced. Baxter first skied on the slopes of Aviemore, at the age of 2. By his mid-teens his talent was recognised, and his dream was to challenge for top honours in the sport. Yet in Britain no funding was available, and so began a ten year slog, driving around Europe, living on overdraft, sleeping in hostels and cheap hotels or in the back of his car.

In 2002, at Salt Lake City Winter Olympics, Baxter caused the biggest upset by clinching Britain's first ever skiing medal. Agonisingly, the ecstasy was short-lived. No sooner had he returned to a hero's welcome than the call came that he had failed a routine drugs test and would be stripped of his medal. Baxter was stunned and mystified.

After Salt Lake there were many dark months as Baxter fought to clear his name and reclaim his medal. For someone who had wanted it so badly, who never wanted anything else, one can only imagine how much that must have hurt. But in his darkest hour came hope. Represented by one of Europe's most respected barristers, and with the backing of the British Olympic Association, Baxter took his fight to sport's highest appeal court. Safe in the knowledge that the tiny trace of Methamphetamine in Baxter's bloodstream had resulted from his innocent use of a US Vicks Inhaler, his legal team went on the offensive.

Sensationally, Baxter was cleared but, despite endorsing the verdict, the IOC was steadfast: Baxter would never get his medal back, though he was welcomed back for the 2006 Olympics. Today Baxter dreams of climbing back up the world rankings to his rightful place, at the top of the tree.

For full details of all our titles
please visit our website at

www.dewilewismedia.com